FROM GERMAN WAR TO JEWISH PEACE

My life journey from the Waffen-SS to Judaism

Yitzchak von Schweitzer

To Natalie

MENSCH PRESS

Enjoy the read

Yitzchak

Mensch Press

https://www.themenschpress.com/

From German War to Jewish Peace

ISBN: 979-8-9861079-4-3

This book is dedicated to my dearest wife Rivka and our family

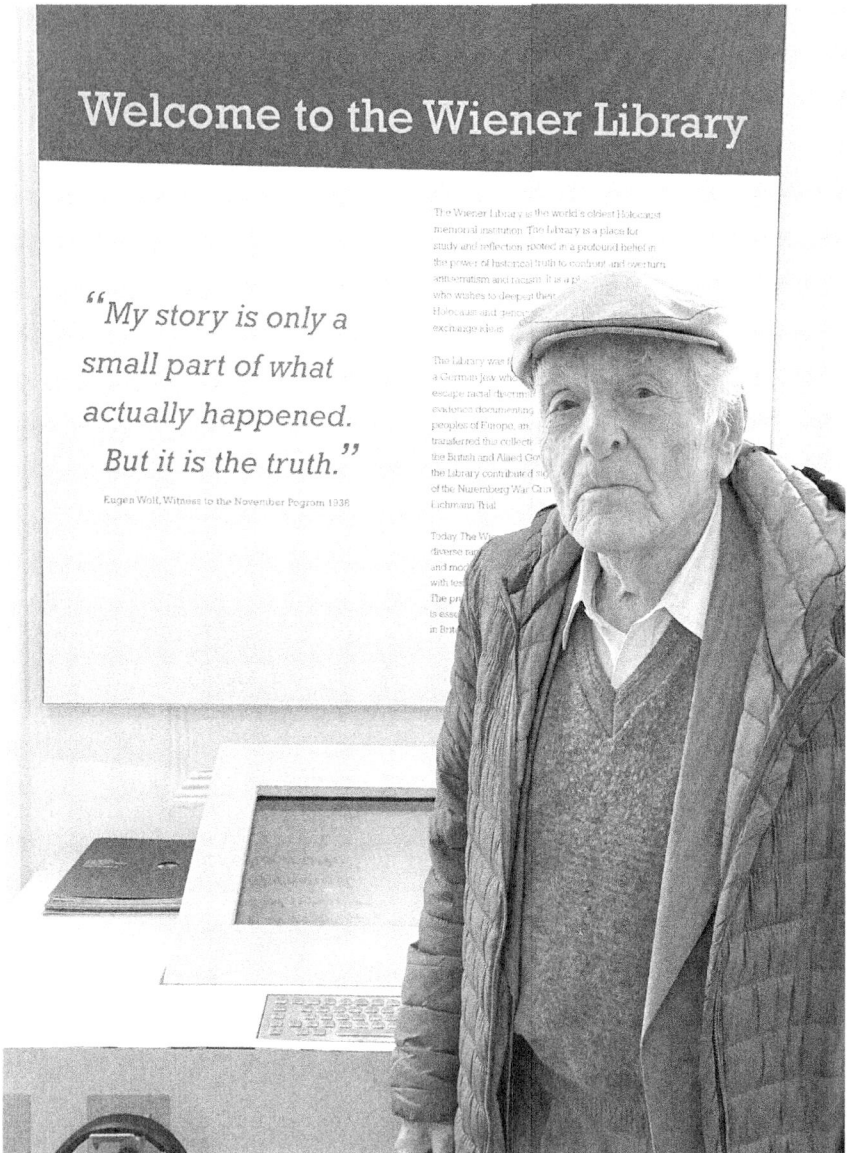

Welcome to the Wiener Library

"My story is only a small part of what actually happened. But it is the truth."

Eugen Wolf, Witness to the November Pogrom 1938

The Wiener Library is the world's oldest Holocaust memorial institution. The Library is a place for study and reflection rooted in a profound belief in the power of historical truth to confront and overturn antisemitism and racism. It is a pl[...] who wishes to deepen their [...] Holocaust and perse[...] exchange ideas [...]

The Library was f[...] a German Jew who [...] escape racial discrimi[...] evidence documenting [...] peoples of Europe, in [...] transferred this collecti[...] the British and Allied Gov[...] the Library contributed no[...] of the Nuremberg War Cri[...] Eichmann Trial [...]

Today The W[...] diverse ra[...] and mo[...] with te[...] The pr[...] is ess[...] in Brit[...]

Figure 1 - Yitzchak at Wiener Holocaust Library, London, February 2023

Acknowledgements

MY THANKS:

TO DR. SERENA GOULD, without whose help and encouragement this would not have been completed.

TO MY SONS Stephen and Karl for their technical and moral support.

TO DAVID RAYNER and his father, Steven, for their technical help and advice.

TO MY SON-IN-LAW, Mark, for his patience whenever I called on him once again with the same computer problems.

TO SCOTT at Snappy Snaps in Edgeware for patiently digitizing the photographs and documents.

Contents

PROLOGUE

TOWARDS THE END of a long life of exploring, I am recounting my experiences of the radical changes that I managed to survive for 96 years at the time of this writing.

Born on Rosh Chodesh Sivan 5687 (May 14, 1926) as the potential Catholic heir to two modest baronial estates in Lower Austria, I am now a British Orthodox-Jewish retired professional and still remain a perpetually questioning student. This extraordinary journey of nearly a century is in part the story of a noble family's survival through the ravages of World War I, inflation, depression, Hitler's rise in Nazi Germany, World War II, and Germany's recovery after 1945. For me, living through all these world-shaking events led to a personal renaissance: in Austria; in Germany before and throughout the war; in London after the war; and, after a short spell in the new Germany, in a more permanent destination in Johannesburg, South Africa. I now find myself back in London with my wife of 55 years, Rivka, surrounded by our daughter, grandchildren, and our Orthodox Jewish community.

A great deal of this life story came about through unlikely events and might easily have gone quite differently. I feel I was born to examine and explore, learning as I went along. Such a search has led me to astonishing, fortuitous, and sometimes even miraculous encounters of survival, upheaval, and radical change, which in and themselves have led to further quests and problems to solve, as well as engagements that have defied the prevailing systems. All of this has made my life forever challenging as I play the role of the 'perpetual outsider'.

In terms of world-shaking events, this included the Great Depression of the 1930s from my rather off-the-beaten-path Austrian childhood perspective, which was swept away by my life in the German Third Reich until 1939, leading to World War II. This period led me to serve in a Waffen-SS fighting unit in 1944, trying to block the Russian advance on Berlin. More rapid transformations in Europe with the Allied victory led to three years of being a prisoner of war in Paderborn, Brussels, and London. After repatriation and a six-month break with my family in the defeated and occupied Germany in 1948, I returned to England to university and marriage in a Labour-governed England.

My 25-year retail career with the John Lewis Partnership (from porter to general manager) included the birth of three children, a divorce, and a second marriage to my wife, Pam. By 1971, England had stagnated at the mercy of domineering unions and, ironically, envied the 'German Miracle' on the other side of the Channel. With my fluent German and understanding of its culture, the ITT conglomerate offered my family and me an 'American' entry to the German-speaking countries on the continent, which included Austria and Switzerland as well as Germany.

The jump to Johannesburg during apartheid South Africa in 1975 with two small children was prompted by South West African family connections and the stress of a roving, never-at-home working life with ITT. After a year in shopping-centre and hotel development, I joined a Jewish family business and remained in Johannesburg up to my official retirement age (65) in 1991. Indefatigable Pam played a growing role in the mostly Jewish clothing industry.

By 1984, we had become full participants in the Orthodox Jewish community in Waverley, Johannesburg. Our two young children graduated very successfully from the leading Jewish high schools to Witwatersrand University. Extramurally, I played a foundational role in the Institute of Internal Auditors in South Africa and beyond. I graduated with an MBA at the Wits Business School and led a volunteer alumni association.

Apartheid was becoming increasingly impossible to live with, and entrepreneurial Pam seized opportunities to first acquire a factory shop, and then production equipment and clothing factories from the large liquidations taking place. We became business owners over the next 20 years, a horrendous time of struggling for survival in the failing Johannesburg clothing industry.

Since our Jewish rebirth, we became part of an astonishing intensification of Jewish life in South Africa. Despite massive emigration, including our own children, the overall community of some 40,000 held on to strongly affiliated Jewish identities, taking us along with this movement.

The 20th century witnessed murder, leveraged to its ultimate levels during the first half, followed by an unprecedented recovery and prosperity during its second half. The 21st century arrived with a volatile start, which has seemed to continue. What is there to remember and learn from such an experience? What can be the verdict from a surviving eyewitness and participant, born in 1926 in Austria, who skirted the edge of a German catastrophe as a teenager in the Hitler Youth and a young soldier in the Waffen SS? How would this play itself out to a home and a new life in post-war London, finally ending up a respectable Orthodox Jew in Johannesburg, South Africa?

What is the truth? For much of my life, I left my Nazi and brief Waffen-SS experience unmentioned and in abeyance as something that could only stir up trouble and rejection for me. After all, what choice did I have? Yet, I did have a choice; several in fact. I could have chosen otherwise with dire consequences. That would have required a boy with more insight, conviction, and courage than I had at that time. Instead, I was adventurous, ambitious, and intent on surviving.

In the end, it is up to all of us (approximately eight billion individuals worldwide as well as future generations) to come up with an understanding of the past that will enable us to envision and create our common survival. We are moving at ever faster paces scientifically and technically. More than ever before, we are becoming aware of the unknown immensity of what else we need to know and understand to encounter our human future. In evolutionary biological terms, we are expanding to become ever more diverse and interrelated humanity, which must work to improve our chances of long-term survival against the unknowable odds ahead. We must become more creative, inventive, and trustworthy for our future survival as humankind.

My family, the Roepke-Schweitzer Clan, made a fair start in the 19th century from Eastern European, Scandinavian, Italian, German, and Austrian roots. It survived the two World Wars of the 20th century as thoroughly defeated and condemned Germans in both cases. It recovered in unexpected ways in the aftermath of those devastating wars. Our family has spread far and wide, and now faces the future with the addition of English, Jewish, Zulu, French, American, Australian, and Sikh descendants. I smile when I contemplate this and my part in these changes, at the same time wondering how my stern patriarchal ancestors would have understood it.

Our family life story has also changed over the generations, from male dominance to female assurance and inclusion. In a wider sense, this personal account of how it all came about for us over the last century is also echoed by all the stories of the families who survived those world-shaking and shocking times.

Family Tree 1

Franz **Maria** Suaizer von Schweitzer (1722 - 1812) - - - - Paula Maria Angela Franziska Allesina (1725 -1791)

Anton Maria Moriz von Schweitzer (1759 - 1829) - - - - Wlhelmina Maria Petronella von Barrazzi (1775 - 1864)

Karl Franz Allesina von Schweitzer (1800 - 1885) - - - - Sofie Antonie Marie von Brentano La Roche (1806 – 1856)

Georg Willhelm Allesina von Schweitzer (1832 - 1897) - - - - Ida Caroline Sophie von Kleyle (1842 – 1917)

Karl Friedrich Maria Allesina von Schweitzer (1863 – 1901) - - - - Sara Ottilia, Countess Wrangel af Sauss (1869 – 1935)

Margaritha von Mossig (1900 – 1930) - - - - **Otto** Bernhard Allesina von Schweitzer (1894 – 1981) - - - - **Ursula** Roepke (1905 – 1998)

Gottfried | **Helmut** | Rosemarie & Irmingard | Peter, Brigitte & Heidi

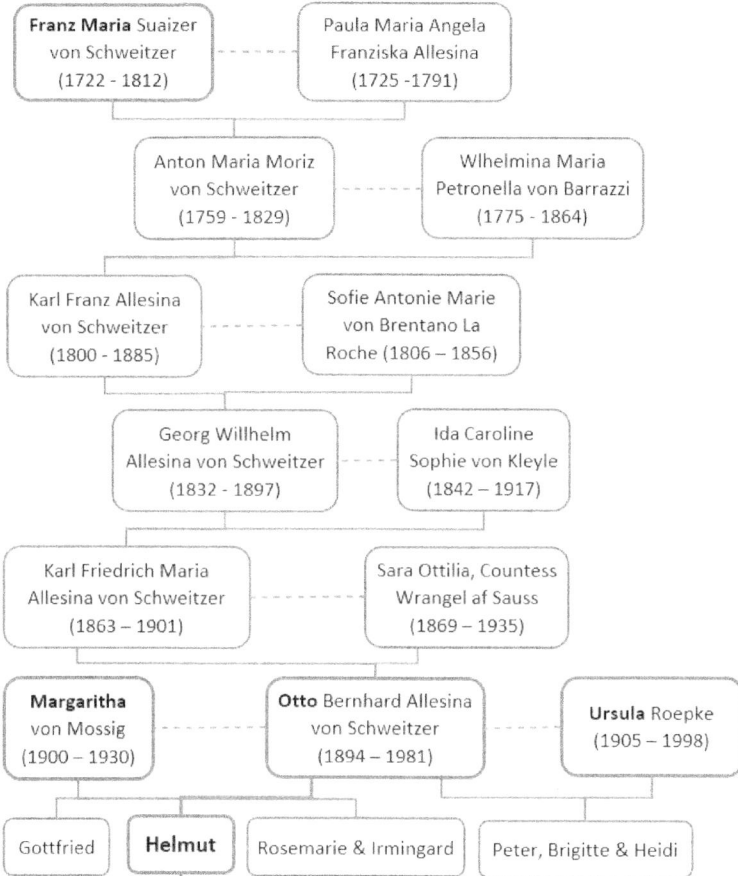

Page 2 to follow

I

Contd from previous page

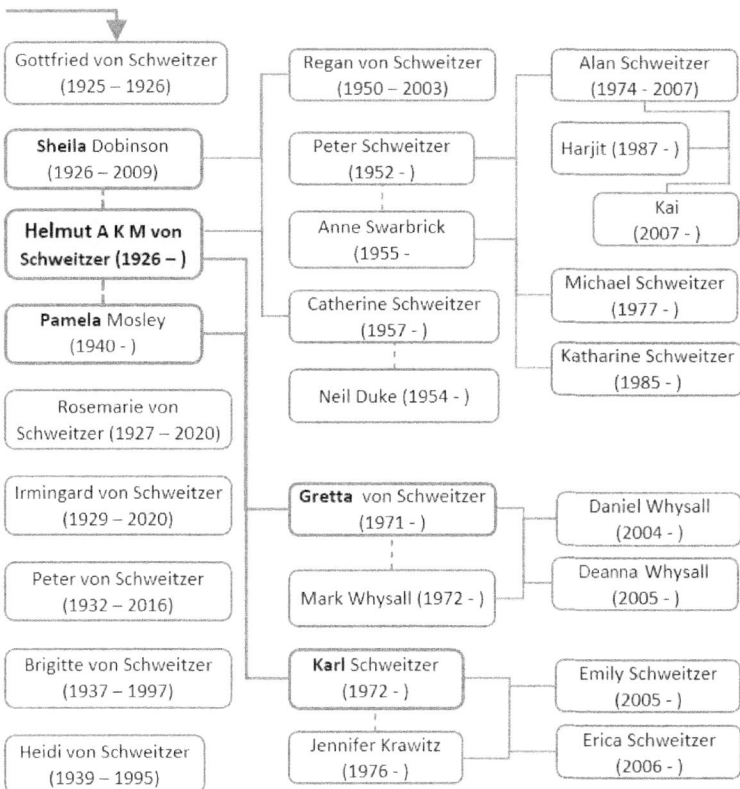

Gottfried von Schweitzer
(1925 – 1926)

Sheila Dobinson
(1926 – 2009)

**Helmut A K M von
Schweitzer (1926 –)**

Pamela Mosley
(1940 -)

Rosemarie von
Schweitzer (1927 – 2020)

Irmingard von Schweitzer
(1929 – 2020)

Peter von Schweitzer
(1932 – 2016)

Brigitte von Schweitzer
(1937 – 1997)

Heidi von Schweitzer
(1939 – 1995)

Regan von Schweitzer
(1950 – 2003)

Peter Schweitzer
(1952 -)

Anne Swarbrick
(1955 -

Catherine Schweitzer
(1957 -)

Neil Duke (1954 -)

Gretta von Schweitzer
(1971 -)

Mark Whysall (1972 -)

Karl Schweitzer
(1972 -)

Jennifer Krawitz
(1976 -)

Alan Schweitzer
(1974 - 2007)

Harjit (1987 -)

Kai
(2007 -)

Michael Schweitzer
(1977 -)

Katharine Schweitzer
(1985 -)

Daniel Whysall
(2004 -)

Deanna Whysall
(2005 -)

Emily Schweitzer
(2005 -)

Erica Schweitzer
(2006 -)

PART I

CHILDHOOD IN GNEIXENDORF

Childhood

LIVING IN OUR Austrian country mansion home, Schloss Gneixendorf, we children were always together in our large, sunny nursery. Little did we know that this was where Composer Ludwig van Beethoven had stayed 100 years before in late 1826. Our salon had served as the Gneixendorf Catholic church until the 19th century. The other main landmark features were the square frontal clock tower and beyond the gardens, the large, ornamented storage building. These structures were already over 300 years old by the time we were there.

I was born in 1926 to Otto Schweitzer and Margeritha (known as Gritta), née Mossig, as their second child, soon the oldest and their only son after the accidental drowning of my older brother, Gottfried, in a water cistern soon after my birth. My church christening was confirmed with the traditional formal family photograph, showing Gottfried alive as a toddler. My birth was followed by my sisters, Rosemarie and Irmingard. This happy family soon suffered the premature death of our dear mother.

In the nursery, our cots stood end-to-end along the inner warmer walls. Our maids, Maria and Mitzi, woke, dressed, washed, and fed us there. Mutti and Dad would come in to see us during the day and for goodnight. Mutti would take us out into the garden to meet friends during the day. Once we were bedded down in our bedroom/playroom in the evening, she would kiss each of us on our forehead as we were falling asleep.

Figure 2 - Helmut Christening, Gneixendorf, 1926

Busy in our large nursery, I was soon heaving around heavy furniture and toys from Dad's childhood. I stacked them up to look, at least to my eyes, like Dad's new combine harvester and tractors in the farmyard or like the castle ruins along the Danube. In the hurly-burly of such effort, the stuffed elephant on metal wheels jammed my left foot, inflicting osteomyelitis, then still incurable. This wound had to be kept open, bathed, and bandaged daily. Doctor Viatoris had me at the hospital in Krems for several operations. When I was brought home before Christmas, I still had an open wound needing daily footbaths and bandages.

Figure 3 - Mutti, Papa, Helmut (On Table) and Baby Rosi

Goodnight Mutti

BABY IRMI WAS born when sister Rosi was two and I nearly four, following the two of us in the family baby cot that Dad had built by himself before any one of us was born, placed in the warm stove corner of our nursery.

Five weeks after Irmi's birth, I was awakened in the middle of one night by Dad in his nightshirt and led to our parents' bedroom. Mutti was lying there on the bed in her white nighty. I bent down, and she kissed me on both cheeks. Not a word was spoken. Dad took me back to my bed. This must have been the night Mutti died, January 21, 1930. We children were not told about it. I would always remember this last farewell. At just under four years old, I would be the only one of us with recallable memories of our Mother.

Gritta Mutti was gone forever. She had died of what had been diagnosed too late by the doctor as blood poisoning. The house staff thought she had been infected by contact with my open foot wound. Sister Irmi never ceased to believe that father blamed her birth, which she thought had led to Gritta Mutti's death. Dad and Irmi would be at loggerheads without ever facing these feelings.

After Gritta Mutti's death, the routines of our lives with the maids continued as before. Now maiden Aunt Tilla, my father's older sister and grandmother Lilli, Father's Swedish-born mother, called *Mutch* by the grownups and *Mamah* by us children, came across from their 'Little House', a double-storey house on the far side of our park-like back garden, to help.

Following the family tradition, set by Great-Grandmother Ida, they had moved out of the main mansion when Father Otto moved in with our Gritta Mutti. Grandmother Lilli and Aunt Tilla were financially dependent on our father for the rest of their lives.

Figure 4 - Mutch, Tilla, Papa, Gritta-Mutti

Finance and business were never talked about in our family; it just was not the 'done thing' in good society. World War I and the ties of country life had given Tilla few chances of a suitable match. The young man who proposed to her was not impressive enough for her brothers, so she rejected his proposal. Tilla became the only real companion for her formidable, long-suffering mother, Lilli, who had been widowed when Tilla was only nine years old. We three little children provided the only real scope for them to take an active part in the family after Mother's tragic death.

Tilla and Mutch (Mama) rose to the challenge, starting from the two-year span 1930-1932 before Father had remarried, creating life-long bonds between us three children and them, stepping into the breach when we children needed it most. Tilla and baby Irmi grew into a mother/daughter-like intimacy. Rosi claimed she was always the 'lonely child in the middle', on her own, but conceded that she may have been her father's favourite child, which he confirmed in a late-life letter to her written for her birthday. Mamah was my inspiration. She made me an Anglophile from the start. In retrospect, she was to be an augury for my future.

Aunt Tilla took Mother's place, spending a lot of time with us and looking after baby Irmi. Tilla also made notes about us, particularly about Irmi's cheerful nature, and details of her gains in weight and awareness. 'Rosi', she wrote, 'was the darling of all the guests, a smiling charmer, but jealous and temperamental. Tilla was the epitome of plain modesty. Helmut was more wayward; he wanted to take all the animals away from the butchers to keep them alive'. Irmi only found these notes after Tilla's death in 1956.

Throughout our lives, we three Gritta children remained unself-consciously and unquestioningly close. Somehow, all these early memories would merge into the spirit of an idealized Gritta mother image growing within us.

Did we miss Mother acutely, cry for her? No - Dad had made sure our daily lives would continue as before. Father would never allow us to talk about it or to mourn. Closed subject. Mother's death must have been a terrible shock for him, particularly because it could have been prevented. How did we find out about all this? Mostly from visiting cousins and some of the staff. Nevertheless, somehow Gritta Mutti never quite left her children.

Dad's approach meant that the children had to move on. Tilla and Mutch had to conform. They disliked gimmicks involving the Easter bunny, Christmas trees, gifts, and celebrations: 'We had happy holiday celebrations in our youth without all such make-believe,' Tilla wrote disparagingly in her diary. Their criticism was directed at Gritta's personality and ways, which had filled the Schloss household with new life, but also the 'bad examples' of her Viennese background, exemplified by her visiting Viennese nieces and nephews.

The prevailing Schweitzer obligation of family peace was always achieved at the cost of unspoken and unresolved tensions. As an example, no issue was made of Uncle Georg's visits when he became an early affiliated Nazi party member and later, after the war, a convicted post-war political criminal. It was just never a 'talking topic'.

As Irmi became Tilla's child, Rosi and I became of one mind to find out all we could about Gritta Mutti. We oriented ourselves by her unremoved wall portraits and any personal items we could detect and collect. We felt our way to her and she to us. Rosi and I drew together as 'Gritta Mutti's kids,' sharing stories and artifacts connected with Gritta Mutti. This was implicit to us for life. Later in our lives, we also found some of her diaries and writings, which revealed what a spiritual and exceptional person she had been. Rosi would always look after Mother's grave and decided to be buried with her, confirming the nearness and love she had found in her first two years.

Our Parents

MOTHER GRITTA (1900-1930) was the eldest of three daughters of the von Mossigs, an Austrian military family. She had been a distinguished scholar at the Sacré-Coeur Residential College in Prague. As an intellectual Catholic, she also turned our father Otto (1894-1981) into a regular churchgoer during her time.

Figure 5 - Gritta-Mutti

Father was the youngest of three children. He had lost his own father, Karl (1863-1901), at the young age of seven. Mother Lilli (1869-1935), our *Mutch* or Mama, had been born Countess Wrangel in Lutheran Sweden. She accepted the conventional Austrian Catholicism for her children but entrusted them to the young, British, Church-of-England Maud as their governess and nanny. Uncle Georg, Aunt Tilla, and Dad were all verbally fluent in English thanks to 'Aunt Maud', who remained a lifelong family friend after she had married the Austrian constructor of the Schweitzer tennis court.

Gritta was the first woman in her family, and later, the Schweitzer family with a high school graduation and a religious dedication. After 1918, she returned from Prague to Vienna as a laureate college graduate. She founded and led a study and discussion group of lively youngsters in Vienna, known as *Der Lesetee* (tea-time studies). They also organized weekend wandering excursions, and read and discussed Dante's *Divine Comedy*, Nietzsche's *Zarathustra* as well as Christian Morgenstern's verses.

Gritta kept notes of what she read from 1919 until the end of 1929. Her rescued reading book diary is dedicated as '*Heilig, Heilig, is das Leben. Ich kann nicht mehr sagen*' (Holy holy is life, all I can say). She made notes after reading the book *The Wrong God*, by Theodor Fritsch, one of the virulently antisemitic writers of the 1920s and 30s. She found it hard to understand his arguments: 'There should be no need to hate when we are faithful to what is good for all of us'. Her book pages contain notes on readings that range widely from poems and novels to psychology, science and philosophy, authors from Plato and Augustine, Strindberg and Lagerlof to Darwin and Freud. Her last sentence in this book was, 'The purpose of being human is learning from the world and God'.

Figure 6 - Gritta-Mutti Portrait, Oil Painting

All the controlled mechanizing and systematizing of the farm gave Otto in Gneixendorf chances to get away for weekends with friends, canoeing on the Danube and socializing in Vienna. His friend, Heinrich, introduced him to Gritta Mossig's *Lesetee* society in Vienna. Like the other men, Otto found Gritta very attractive. Gritta made her choice on an outing to the Schneeberg (Snow Mountain) on June 17, 1923. We children could see the Schneeberg faintly from our nursery on clear days in the distant south.

Her engagement to Dad led to the production of an insightful and fun pre-wedding musical drama in Vienna, alluding to Schiller's *Wilhelm Tell* drama. Gritta Mutti's own surviving 20-page typed text of this inspired satirical musical show became a revelation to us when we found it after Dad's death in 1981.

During their engagement, Otto and Gritta arranged a *Lesetee* hike of the Wachau section of the Danube, to culminate with high tea at Otto's home in Schloss Gneixendorf. Tilla met the party early on Sunday morning as they arrived from Vienna at the nearby Krems rail station. Here she met Gritta for the first time as well as her father Alfred, who had also come along with the party. Tilla walked home alone, disappointed as the party promptly dispersed for church services and foraging. She had to go back to see to the high tea preparations.

After the party had arrived in good spirits at the mansion in the early evening, Tilla disapproved of Gritta's friends and their free conduct, writing in her diary that Otto should not marry Gritta. Tilla continued her diary writing for most of her life, and her writings were found long after her death; they expressed her innermost feelings even when she could not do so publicly, afraid of angering those around her due to her dependent position in the family.

Gritta introduced an active Catholic and intellectual life to the otherwise placid and tolerant Schloss Gneixendorf. Her contribution to solving the financial problems of running the estate was to have paying guests who would enjoy the ambience of this serene, baroque mansion.

Gritta Mutti also introduced the brown-leather gold-rimmed guestbook reflecting her artistic Viennese links, filled with messages, drawings, poems, and ditties that were a kaleidoscope of the stream of visitors to our past home, beginning with the *Polterabend*, eve-of-wedding party in Vienna on November 14, 1923.

Figure 7 - Family Guest Book, Cover

All kinds of guests contributed to this book — family, friends and paying guests — but 'friends all together' according to the book's testimony. This book would continue to serve the family for many years, closing with Dad's funeral.

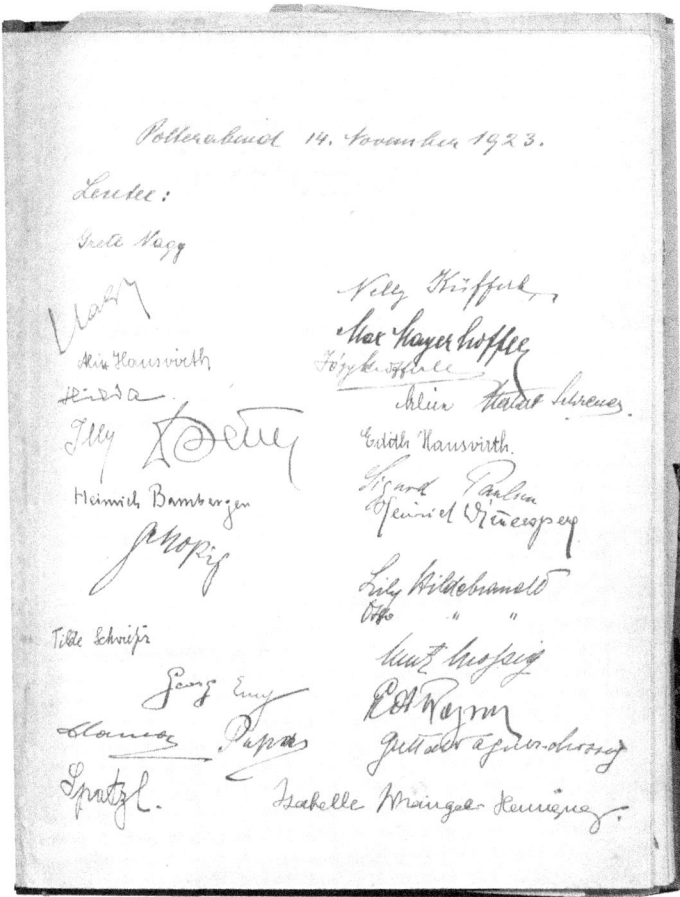

Figure 8 - Family Guest Book: First inside page

Growing Up In Gneixendorf

ROSI AND I managed more or less on our own together. We children had to find our own answers and solutions, learning by trial and error. For me, it meant getting out on the street to be with the village kids, where everybody talked as straight as they liked. I was to them the *Schweitzer-Kaas*; all cheeses on sale in the village shop were 'Schweizer (Swiss) Kaese'.

We upper-village boys were often at loggerheads with the boys from the main lower village, against whom we had stone-throwing battles when they intruded on our area.

On exploratory wanderings with the other kids and often on our own, we always anticipated problems with people and guard dogs. Once we clambered down the banks of the vineyards to the Danube valley. We put our ears to the train rails and heard a rumbling sound. When the train chuff-chuffed past us, I was shocked by the boxy carriages looking nothing like the window carriages of my toy train at home.

We kids kept away from the villages, particularly Stratzing and even lower Gneixendorf. I liked rambling around our countryside on my own for hours on end. I would make sure to come back home with a bunch of wildflowers for Mamah and Tilla, and also for us. My top-secret spot was the wild orchids on the Galgen(gallows)berg. Picking these rare 'Ladies' Slippers' was outlawed.

The other secret along the same stretch of the old, straight Roman Road was the forgotten Krems Jewish cemetery, which was completely overgrown in bushes and nettles. We kids had no idea what it really was, but for me, it later became a pointer to the many precursors of a Jewish presence in my life.

Being out with the grown-ups was, of course, quite different. It meant walking tidily dressed and steadily in order, particularly through the villages, where the adults would exchange polite greetings. Dad was the mayor of Gneixendorf, and people would still greet him as 'Herr Baron', despite the government having already abolished all titles.

One winter, three of us boys were chasing down the slope of the next-door Kneifl pond onto the flat ice surface, using the heavy sledge from Dad's childhood. The ice cracked in the middle. We were sinking into the depths. I grabbed the ice's surface edge before me and crawled onto it. We all got off soaked and ran home. Our parents were upset about our 'adventure'. The Kneifls locked us out from their pond area.

Dad might have been reserved, but he could also rise to loud fury. One day, he had taken Rosi and me to the lilac bushes in our South Garden to hidden homemade sheds with six white hares. He also showed us their food and water containers. He then left us behind. Days later, he had us there again, shouting at us. He had expected us to feed and look after these orphaned hares. We had not realised that he wanted us to do it or how to do it from now on. He stormed out of this garden section, locking us in. Rosi was crying desperately, and I did my best to calm her. Dad opened the garden gate in time for supper. When we checked the bushes the following afternoon, the hares and their boxes had disappeared, never to be mentioned again.

Tilla wrote in her diary, 'Otto is not close enough to his children. When playing Helmut always takes charge. Perhaps he will also take charge in marriage, which cannot be said at all about his father'.

When Grandmother Mamah was reading to us, it was from her Swedish Hans Andersen and Selma Lagerlöf books. I also remember tracing a map of England for her as a surprise birthday present, with all the in-and-out endless coastlines, before I had even learned to write.

Uncle Georg, Dad's older brother, arrived at the birthday party shouting, 'Goodah Goodah!' 'Hi Hello' in Swedish. He was the one who read English detective stories that he ordered by special post from England. Uncle Georg was the family intellectual. Dad, on the other hand, was not a party person. He was always doing things and would then let the results speak for themselves. This was all summed up in the final sentence of Mamah's diary in 1932: 'My children Georg and Tilde I do understand, but Otto is beyond me'.

Ulla Mutti Arrives

AND THEN OUR dad did it again.

Dad reported back to our assembled family in our nursery in 1931 that he was engaged to marry the lovely Ulla Roepke from Germany, who would become our mother. I jumped up with my favourite volume of fairy tales and handed it to him as my present for her. He took it to her in Germany and came back with a beautifully illustrated, mighty pictorial fairy tale volume from her, almost too large for Tilla to hold when she was reading to us.

Within two years, we had our energetic, resourceful German Ulla Mutti as our mother. Dad could not have found a more capable wife to take charge of him and our family in the coming years.

Ulla Mutti had become our mother with a Lutheran Roepke wedding in Melsungen, Germany, and a formal Catholic wedding in Linz, Austria in February 1932. Dad did not expose the family to a possibly controversial Gneixendorf family wedding.

Ursula was the eldest child of Professor Doctor Otto Roepke and his wife Margarethe. Ulla had graduated from university as a Home Science lecturer, as the first woman graduate in her family. It had been love at first sight. Her father, Otto, was not going to let Ulla wed this odd Austrian father of three little children, and a Catholic to boot! But Ulla stood her ground, backed by the rest of her family.

The newlyweds arrived in Gneixendorf with a bevy of young folk, college friends, and siblings. Our place became a hive of activity, and

Ulla Mutti managed it all with cheerful vigour and enterprise.

Father and Ulla Mutti were both hands-on practical people, working well together. Among all the new equipment she brought with her was a manual fruit press, ideal for all the apples and pears from the trees planted by great Grandfather Karl along the kilometre-long, straight tracks between the fields. Her apple juice was on the table all year round. Now pigs were raised and slaughtered during the winter, and the meat was canned with her equipment, providing convenient ready-canned meat and sausages all year round.

Ulla Mutti fitted in with all the Austrian relationships and even strengthened some. Her nature and interests were direct and practical. No more servants in the home. Father's resolute closure of the past did open a new beginning. The Great Depression raised very urgent new demands. Doctor's daughter, Ulla Mutti, was always in charge at home, and she knew how to deal with medical problems and when to call Doctor Viatoris from Krems. She was also the first mother anywhere around in Austria to have her first baby, our half-brother Peter, in the Krems hospital, and not at home.

Our Home Becomes
a Gathering Place

SCHLOSS GNEIXENDORF HAD become the holiday resort of the wider family. Paying guests were welcome. 'Aunt' Berta Ruck, the popular novelist from England, would stay for weeks every summer to dictate her next novel to a secretary she brought with her. She eventually published more than 100 novels.

Figure 9 - Picture of Berta Ruck

Years later, after the war while being a POW in London in 1947, I did write to her at her home in Wales. She replied promptly, inviting me to join her at the Café Royal on Regent Street at her next stay in town. As a German POW bomb disposal camp leader, I got my pass from our camp to travel to Piccadilly to meet her. Nobody stopped me from entering this exclusive, elegant Café Royal in my patched POW uniform. To my own consternation and the astonishment of the other guests in this society café, Aunt Berta rushed up to me and embraced me as a long-lost friend. She had last seen me in Gneixendorf as a dreamy eight-year-old, twelve years before! We met then whenever she came up to town.

Father had astonishing friends as regular visitors to Schloss Gneixendorf, particularly Kurt and Martha Beindorf from Hanover and Uncle Heinrich Wimmersperg from Vienna. Uncle Kurt and Dad had teamed up in Siberia as Russian prisoners of war in World War I.

They managed to survive together. Kurt, from Hanover, was a technocrat and Aunt Martha, our most lively and generous aunt, was heir to the Pelikan Werke, the leading German producer of writing utensils, inks, and paints. She also headed the German Ladies' car racing club. Ulla Mutti and Aunt Martha became close friends.

More astonishing perhaps was Father's equally enduring friendship with Uncle Heinrich, Count Wimmersperg, the genial inventor from Vienna, originally a founding member of Gritta's *Lesetee*. He had an original angle on everything he touched and was a particularly creative do-it-yourself photographer. Whilst Uncle Heinrich struggled to sell his inventions, including quick-firing handguns, he spent a great deal of his time with us in Gneixendorf. Here he met and soon married Aunt Frances, Berta Ruck's USA-born secretary. They would always remain our family friends.

He claimed to have invented the safety airbags for cars, but had been unable to fund the necessary patents, prototypes, and litigation to secure his legal rights to such an application-variant concept. After Hitler's annexation of Austria in 1938, Uncle Heinrich was absorbed into the small arms program for the German army. Following the German defeat in 1945, Frances and Heinrich were whisked away to the United States as part of the US operation 'Paperclip', cornering the best German brains for the USA. They became an unfailing source of care parcels for our family in the hungry early post-war years.

Our parents never had to go to a village school in their youth, but from September 1932, I was at the single-form village primary school. When Rosi followed me in 1933, she did her best to get me to concentrate. All written work was done on slates: one side for writing, the other for arithmetic. Once our teacher had checked the homework and the sides had been wiped clean, the slate was ready for the next day and tasks. For manual writing, we were taught the now forgotten angular German alphabet. At that time, the more regular Roman letter writing was only learned in high school in the foreign language classes.

Our years in Gneixendorf were trying but fulfilling, thanks to our mothers, Dad, Tilla and Mutch, as well as the wider family and local friends.

PART 2

OUR FAMILY HISTORY

Founding

OUR FAMILY WAS founded in 1751 by 29-year-old Dr. Juris Francisco Maria Suaicara's arrival in the Imperial Free City of Frankfurt-am-Main. Originating from Verona, Francisco was a new and ambitious addition to the longstanding colony of enterprising Italian traders tolerated by the city. Francisco had registered on arrival as Herr Suaicar. In his application for citizenship, he Germanized his name to Franz Suaitzer. His citizenship was only granted after 15 years of procrastination by the city council. He married Paula Allesina, the only child of the wealthy Allesina family, as Italian families tended to stick together and intermarry among themselves. He rose from managing his wife's family textile business to owning the growing enterprise.

By the time Franz gained his citizenship 15 years later, our family name had already become Allesina von Schweitzer. He was ennobled by the Catholic King Ludwig of Bavaria, who always needed funding for his grand, picturesque castles around his kingdom.

Ironically, Franz' past was conveniently reinvented for him by the German authorities later during the Nationalistic German phase in the mid-18th century, with a mythical German grandfather named 'Schweikhart' who had apparently come to Verona from his *real* origins in Germany and had his family name abbreviated in Italy to Suaicara.

Francisco, now Franz Maria, was a born leader. He ran what may have been the second-most successful business in the city during the Napoleonic years, trading in French and Oriental silks. Unofficially, the most successful business must have been the by-then undercover Rothschild international financing from the Jewish ghetto around the corner from the Catholic cathedral in the city centre.

By the time of the French Revolution in 1789, Franz had become Privy-Councillor of the King of Bavaria, with the title '*Allesina genannt von Schweitzer*'. Money talks. For almost sixty years, he remained one of the most publicly respected figures of his time. The intermarrying Italians (the Brentanos and von Schweitzers) also became the co-founders of Frankfurt as the enduring financial hub of Germany, which has continued until today. The city, with its mighty cathedral, remained a major Roman Catholic outpost. Most inhabitants were by then Lutherans, like the Goethe family.

The Reign of Franz Maria

IN AN AGE when human lives were shorter, a golden wedding was truly exceptional. Franz' in- laws, Paula's parents, Johann and Francisca Allesina, celebrated theirs on May 30, 1774. Son-in-law Franz was just the man to turn this occasion into a grand social celebration. All guests received a golden-wedding memorial silver coin/medal to mark the occasion.

Young advocate Goethe, a youthful playmate of the Schweitzer sons, was one of the guests. Twelve years later, the now-poet Goethe was arrested in Italy as a suspected spy while sketching a fortress. In this pre-passport world, he was able to save himself from prison by producing his Allesina golden wedding memorial coin as his identity. He was released.

The Schweitzer *palais*, built on the new Frankfurt boulevard, *Die Zeil*, between 1784 and 1787, was described by Goethe as 'built in a genuine, solid great Italian style, likely to remain unique'. Goethe even recommended the design of the windows to the Court of Weimar.

Franz was a generous host. His hospitality was 'first come, first served', unusual for that era. His Italian *gelati* were much admired. He sponsored Mozart's concert program during the crowning of the new Habsburg Emperor in the Imperial City of Frankfurt in 1791. Mozart was by then out of favour at the Viennese court in view of his controversial operas *Figaro* and *Così fan Tutte*. Mozart wrote to his father how grateful he was for Schweitzer's personal support for his Frankfurt Coronation concert program.

The Napoleonic reign and wars followed. Franz was a leading nego-
tiator in saving the city from getting ransacked. The French armies
never entered Frankfurt, but Emperor Napoleon had to be financially
reconciled. At his last audience with the Emperor in Paris in 1808,
Franz reportedly had to endure Napoleon furiously screaming at him
about the hostility of the German journals.

Franz and Paula had 14 children. Only five survived him. He died
in 1812 at the age of 90, while Napoleon lost his army during the
Russian winter.

The Schweitzer Family Painting

UNTIL MY GENERATION, there had been an unfailing tradition in our family founder's lineage that the 1758 original almost life-sized oil painting of Founder Franz Maria, his wife, and his then four children (size 173 cm x 111cm), would be passed on to the eldest surviving Schweitzer son from generation to generation. It came to me on the death of Father Otto in 1981.

This painting was restored in Frankfurt and came with us to Johannesburg, South Africa, where it remained until 2013. By then, the renewed Frankfurt Historical Museum was ready as its future home. Our founding family painting has graced the renewed Frankfurt City Museum since 2013.

In this picture, Franz and Paula are impressively decked out in the finest laces, silks, satins, and velvets, embellished and adorned with embroidered motifs and a pearl choker worth a king's ransom around Paula's neck.

Figure 10 - Family Picture of Franz-Maria Von Schweitzer and Family

After his death, Franz' mourning family installed an extravagant outsized marble memorial in the Frankfurt Cathedral. An air raid in WWII split it in two. The post-war restoration replaced it with a miniature replica on the main choir's North wall, which remains today.

Franz' eldest sons served as officers in the French and Russian armies, respectively. Our forebears' youngest son, Anton, became mayor of the city of Frankfurt. The family business continued until 1820.

The Schweitzer grand *palais* was later sold and transformed into the luxury hotel, *Russischer Hof*, hosting kings and potentates during the next 50 years when they stayed in Frankfurt, including the then King of England. *Fürst* Bismarck had wanted it as the Prussian embassy, but later, when Prussia annexed the city in 1866, this foreign 'Italian *palais*' was replaced by the central post office building.

Berlin has precariously survived on and off as the German capital, but Central Frankfurt, with the largest railway station and airport, has grown up without fuss to become the financial capital of the European Community.

Schweitzers and Wrangels

ON THE SCHWEITZER side, interesting characters and stories abound.

Swedish Count Carl Gustav von Wrangel (1839-1917) distinguished himself in the Austrian- Italian wars, but had an affair with Julie, his Regimental Commander's daughter. In view of Julie's pregnancy, her father, Baron von Ripp, laid down the law: 'Resign from Imperial service, marry Julie outside Austria, retire with her to Sweden and never return'. Carl Gustav obeyed orders. Their second child would be our grandmother, Sara Ottilie (Lilli), born in Sweden in 1869: Julie and Carl Gustav had an unhappy marriage. After a Swedish divorce, Mother Julie returned to Vienna with her three children.

On the other side, generous Great Grandmother Ida (1842-1917) was the only child of the late Austrian Imperial Treasurer, Carl Ritter von Kleyle. Ida's grandfather, Dutch Dr. Carl van Mertens, as a physician of the reigning

Figure 11 - Grandmother Sara Ottilia (Lilli), Countess Wrangel

Russian Empress, had persuaded the empress to outlaw all kissing of church icons during a Plague pandemic. All Russia rose in protest at such an 'outrageous' law. Our ancestor Doctor had to save his life, escaping from this danger to Vienna.

In 1863, this same future great grandmother, Ida von Kleyle, married the ambitious Georg Wilhem Allesina von Schweitzer (1832-1897) at St. Stephen's Cathedral in Vienna, to live thereafter at Schloss Gneixendorf, her estate, situated 70km west of Vienna. Baby Karl, our grandfather, was born there on December 8, 1863.

Now the Schweitzer family in Gneixendorf faced their 'Wrangel problem' when Grandfather-to-be Karl introduced his bride, Lilli Wrangel. 'Impossible', said his father, Georg: 'She is penniless. Her parents are divorced. She is a Lutheran, all unacceptable in our Austrian Catholic Imperial society'!

Figure 12 - Tilla, Georg (centre), Otto von Schweitzer (circa 1900)

Grandfather Karl then acquired Schloss Lengenfeld, about 5km northwest of Gneixendorf.

After Grandfather Karl and Grandmother Lilli married in Vienna in August 1890, Grandmother Ida handed her complete Gneixendorf estate to the young couple. There, Karl and Lilli, our grandparents, produced my father and his siblings: Georg Karl, born in 1891 (Uncle Georg); Mathilde Julie, born in 1892 (Aunt Tilla); and Otto Bernhard, born in 1894 (our father).

Grandfather Karl and Grandmother Lilli's happy marriage was cut short by Father Karl's early death in 1901.

Grandma Lilli brought her children up in Gneixendorf and in the neighbouring city, Krems, during the winters, bringing young, educated Maud from London to look after the children.

Figure 13 - Schloss Gneixendorf (circa 1900)

First World War: Father Otto And Uncle Georg

GEORG (23) AND Otto (20) joined their Austrian cavalry regiments to banish the Russian armies to Siberia.

Ensign Otto's cavalry squadron charged boldly into the Russian Ukraine. By the middle of October, Otto's squadron found itself surrounded by Cossack forces. They surrendered. The prisoners were transported to officer POW camps at the far Eastern stretch of the Siberian Railway.

Mother Lilli's diary of the war years is all about her concern over Otto's Russian captivity in Siberia. The occasional Red Cross letters from him took up to six months to get delivered, and all said he was well. After he returned in 1920, Lilli sat down with him to recall and record his Russian ordeal. The resulting pile of handwritten copy books only came to light for us children to read after Dad's death in 1981.

Brother Lieutenant Georg was wounded in 1916, and then he made a deal with a War Office general in Vienna to become a liaison officer with the allied Turkish army in Constantinople. In return, the general's family had free stays at Gneixendorf.

In 1918, on a tram in Vienna, Georg was captivated by the sight of a beautiful dark-haired seamstress. He proposed to her. They married. Tilla would write in her diary: 'Not our kind'. However, our aunt Emmy became a truly stalwart family member. Georg and Emmy had no children.

The Russian surrender in March 1918 included the release of all prisoners of war, but the civil war in the by-then Soviet Russia stalled their return home for another 30 months. Masses of nominal ex-prisoners of war were moving West along the Siberian Railway line as (and when) the raging civil war between the Reds and Whites made it possible. Whenever he had mentioned his Siberian time to us children, Father had told us about the pranks he and 'Uncle' Kurt pulled in their officers' camp. Their practical work was objected to as 'unbecoming' for officers, but otherwise proved very helpful all around. Otto and Kurt became lifelong friends. They had saved each other's lives through illness and starvation as a team to make window shutters for Siberian farmhouses and improvised camp theatre stages with their self-made tools.

Even then, officers such as Otto and Kurt risked getting arrested in Moscow by the ruling Communists of the post-Revolutionary period if they were spotted as 'officer types'.

By the end of the war, the Gneixendorf farm had become the only source of livelihood for the Schweitzer family. Any real turnaround had to wait for Otto's return from the East.

Post-World War I Life

Our father, Otto, had wanted to become a farmer since boyhood. Now he had the onerous task of taking it up in an emergency, without prior technical training. He recalled: 'I had to start without any working capital or cattle, but with fields full of weeds, impoverished by lack of fertilisers'.

Otto would transform a pre-war era farming operation to technical farming with tractors and combine harvesters with money from the bank. There was nothing like it in Europe at that time. As a young boy, I remember admiring Father's mechanized farming, American style, among the first in Europe. People came from far and wide to see this agricultural wonder, managed by Dad's small team of six men. In a second phase, Dad added American-style chicken and egg farming with electric breeding ovens in our cellars. All this proved excitingly productive but not profitable enough to save the Gneixendorf estate during the upcoming Great Depression.

Nil Desperandum (Never Despair) had been the family motto adopted by founder Franz in the 18th century, together with an eagle and a bear in our coat of arms. In reality, *Nil Desperandum* has since been the key to the family survival of his descendants in our times.

Figure 14 - Von Schweitzer Coat of Arms

The Beethoven Gneixendorf Memorial Controversy

A SMALL, WHITE marble bust of the great Beethoven had looked down on us children from the top of the white wardrobe in our nursery at Schloss Gneixendorf. We kids were hardly aware of it. Beethoven had stayed there 100 years before us as a guest of his brother, Johann, who then owned our family home, the then-called *Schloss Wasserhof*. The nearby city of Krems' Music Society endorsed this Beethoven legend with a stone memorial at the spinney of the upper crossroads corner, where we kids would play hide-and-seek games as we grew up. However, I had my own Beethoven story.

Figure 15 - My Bust of Ludwig Van Beethoven

All grown-ups in the village rested on Sunday afternoons. One hot summer Sunday afternoon in 1933, as a seven-year-old, I was frustrated, wandering around outside. Behind their forbidding outer gate, our Kneifl neighbours had a flock of geese that would descend screaming up to the gate if one rattled the gate bars. I was always tempted to do that just for the geese spectacle.

This Sunday, I was startled when the side gate opened, and old Herr Kneifl beckoned me to come in. Was he going to beat me for disturbing their Sunday afternoon rest? No, he was friendly, although our families were not on speaking terms.

Prior to World-War I, Herr Kneifl's carpenter grandfather had furnished an elaborate period-style Beethoven apartment in his house, claiming that this was where Beethoven had actually stayed when he visited his younger brother in 1826. Beethoven sites always attract visitors from all over the world. He advertised and charged entry fees.

The Schweitzers detested commercialism. We, ourselves, occasionally experienced visitors driving up in big, flashy American cars, asking to see 'the Beethoven room'. They quickly left, embarrassed when they were shown into our first-floor nursery by our maid Mitzi, with only the bust of Beethoven perched on top of the wardrobe as evidence of the connection. Shown up to our nursery, they would stand there at the open door, looking at us and our messy toy-strewn nursery, baffled, and soon left.

What they had expected must have been more like the Kneifl show, accompanied by a guide's story. The rooms across the way at the Kneifls must have looked so much more authentic to them.

Herr Kneifl now ushered me inside their house, and then upstairs into a dark-panelled room with old-fashioned furniture and a baby grand piano. This was their 'Beethoven suite', looking like a museum, much more 'real' than our own 'Beethoven room' nursery. We had a real grand piano at home, but it stood in our salon. Our mansion was the 'Schloss' with the big bell tower. Our father was 'Herr Baron von Schweitzer', not a Beethoven guide. Our family condemned the Kneifls for their fake claim and cash-greedy entrance fees but refrained from legal action.

As Herr Kneifl let me out at the gate, we shook hands. He whispered to me, 'You don't have to tell your dad about it'.

I was sure that Dad knew best anyway and certainly did not talk to him about it. It might have upset him. I could do without that. Old Kneifl and I would now greet each other with a conspiratorial winking of our eyes when we met in the village.

American Alexander Thayer (1817-1897) had dedicated his research to Beethoven's life and work. He must have visited Gneixendorf in the early 1850s, describing it as a 'mean hamlet'. Carl von Kleyle, our ancestor, was then an estate owner and the mayor of the village. Thayer described 'two houses, both large and handsome, each with its garden and outer wall, separated by a road. Beethoven's room had a magnificent view of the Danube valley stretching to the distant Styrian mountains'. This was just like the view from our nursery, which confirmed the truth of our Beethoven pilgrimage site.

Thayer's historical facts were that Johann von Beethoven, the composer's younger brother, had been a successful pharmacist who became rich by supplying the medical needs of the rival armies during the Napoleonic wars. He bought the Schloss in 1819.

Beethoven's visit from Vienna had been anything but an easy family get-together. Emotional outbursts and arguments among all family members were the order of the day, all written down as conversations with the by-then totally deaf composer and his nephew, Karl. Ludwig and Karl hastened back to Vienna from Gneixendorf on Saturday, December 2, 1826, with Ludwig in a high dudgeon, riding on the only available vehicle: an open horse-drawn milk cart. Ludwig never recovered from the two-day wintry return trip to Vienna, where he caught a cold and died on March 26, 1827.

PART 3

In Germany 1935-1940

Germany: Our Early Years 1935-6

ULLA-MUTTI FOUND GERMAN solutions for Father's losing battle with farming income in the dissolute Austria of the Great Depression. Our move to Hitler's Germany in 1935 had our family packed into the express train from Vienna to Frankfurt at the start of the summer school holidays.

Since 1934, our parents had been searching in Germany for a suitable farm. The Gneixendorf estate was then sold as a prestige object to a prosperous Viennese family of paint products. We would stay with Mutti's father's family, the Roepkes, in Melsungen. Mamah and Tilla would wait in Austria with Uncle Georg until they could join us directly on our new farm.

What a wonderful adventure for me as a nine-year-old, a train-loving lad who had lived miles away from the railway lines. Now we were returning to our ancestral family home city of Frankfurt.

Our luggage filled the whole train compartment. From my window seat, I could watch how fast we were travelling. We were already on a German train: it was, naturally, running on time.

Rosi was nursing her baby doll, which she adored. Unusually for Europe at that time, her doll was a dark coffee colour with no hair, like a newborn. It had been given to her on her birthday by baby Schmidt, our Hungarian Jewish family friend back in Gneixendorf.

Now Ulla Mutti unwrapped an expensive white doll with blond braids and blue eyes for Rosi. She told her they really wanted her to give up her dark-skinned doll in exchange for this lovely white doll. Rosi insisted on keeping her favorite baby. Mutti tried to persuade her; Father joined in. She would have none of it. Then suddenly Dad just grabbed the black doll and put it away. Rosi was crying bitterly. I was dumbfounded and speechless. Rosi would never touch the new doll. To the end of her life, she would still recall her horror of this experience.

We were then about to stop in Passau on the German border and learned that the German border police would probably have confiscated the 'undesirable' dark-skinned doll. We would certainly have made a bad impression with the German authorities. We already had to prove our racial purity according to the standards of the German Reich, with papers going back over four family generations.

In Germany, everything had to look 'more right' than in dear old Austria, and it often did. It was such a strictly tidy place. Even dolls had to conform to the Aryan ideal.

Another similar document was the Ahnenpass provided by the church, likewise inscribed with the family lineage for generations and stamped by the church. Both these passes necessitated rigorous checking by the government and church authorities.

Fig 19: The document shown here, called an Ahnenpass, was proof of lineage as far back as could be traced, at minimum two generations, to prove no Jewish ancestors. This was verified by the Reich government and stamped on each page. There was a similar one created for the church.

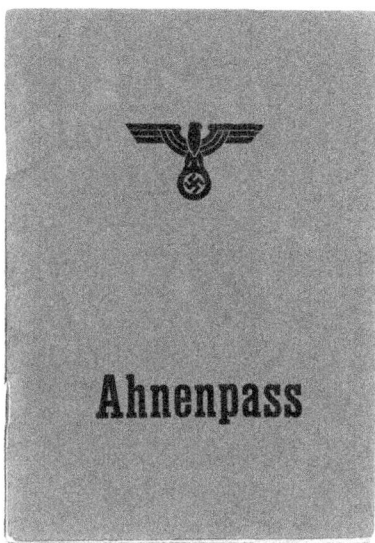

Figure 20 - German Ahnenpass (Cover)

Figure 19 - Sample Inside Page of Ahnenpass

The New Germany with
Grosspapa Roepke – 1935-36

AS A FAMILY, we joined Germany at an opportune time in 1935. Germany meant to become the proud home of all ethnic Germans, joined in the new 'Third Reich'. We stayed at the home of Mutti's doctor father, Otto Roepke, 'Professor Doctor Onkel Grosspapa' to us (The *onkel* was a reminder that we were not blood grandchildren). We had become part of Ulla Mutti's wider family. Grosspapa personified a solid, established Germany that had everything figured out and knew that it was right. He had come from a Prussian village that was now part of Poland. Like our own ancestor, Franz Maria, he had had to prove himself as an outsider to become successful in his profession as a leading German medical lung specialist and head of the major lung clinic.

Germany seemed to us to be so ordered and certain. You could also see this at the big parent Roepke place, the director's villa near the lung sanatorium in the fresh air on a wooded hill above the town of Melsungen.

We stayed there for the summer school holidays and beyond. We saw our parents only at weekends: during the week, they were fixing up our new farm, Wallbachsmuehle, some 20km away, which had to be finished before we could all move in.

Being organised was the German way. Everybody had their definite routine. Professor Onkel Doctor Grosspapa was a role model. He was always impeccably dressed and would only be back at the big house at fixed times. Knowledgeable Grossmama Margarethe was running her home hands-on, doing things herself. If she saw any of us kids at a loose end, she would always have a job for us to do and a treat for us if we did it well, mitigating the strict household way with her implicit kindness.

The whole top of this forest mountain, with the Fulda River and the town of Melsungen down on the north side was a tidy park with walkways. Grosspapa was in charge of everything, and the large clinic ran like clockwork. On the sunny south slope were the terraces of patient rooms and open-air facilities. This being the German railways lung sanatorium, it was always full of train drivers and firemen, sick from their constant exposure to carbon from coal. Each patient had their separate prescribed open-air exercises to clear their lungs.

Grosspapa had two doctors to assist him, but the most important person in the sanatorium (after Grosspapa, of course) was the mighty head nurse, Sister Vera. She looked the part in her white flowing head-nurse garments.

For Rosi, Irmi, and me, it was strange that our parents' names, Otto and Margaritha, were the same as Ulla Mutti's parents' names. The two Ottos, Father and Grosspapa, were both short, broad-shouldered, stocky, and clean-shaven serious men. They were not great talkers but rather more hands-on. They knew their stuff, and we knew to respect and not disturb them. They formally respected each other but never sought out each other's company. Grosspapa Otto had opposed his favourite daughter's choice of husband. The only person who could stand up to him was, fortunately for us, his eldest child, Ulla.

Grosspapa had expected all his children to become medical doctors.

He had made a 'girl exception' for Ulla's household-management teaching career. Heinz and Juergen had qualified, but sons Otto and Wolfgang were not up to it; they would lose their lives as volunteer soldiers on the Russian Front during the future war, as did so many others. Daughter Ilse qualified as a doctor after the war. Wolfgang, the youngest at 18, was still in high school in Melsungen at this time when we were staying there.

After he came back from school on his bike in the afternoon, Wolfgang would always be reading his book (and not doing his homework). No one was allowed to touch the book in his absence. When he had finally finished reading it, he gave it to me, saying, 'It's a good read'. I had never read a grown-up book, and this had 345 pages and no pictures: *Der Schatz im Silber See* (The Treasure in the Silver Lake) by Karl May. It was a Wild-West adventure story, with red Indians and white trappers. I was gripped with excitement. It took me more than two weeks of intense reading to get through it. Now I had to tell the story to my sisters. They were willing listeners when we were sent to bed at 8 pm in the evenings, and the sun was still up.

Now I had to get some more Karl May books to read and retell. The grown-ups around us turned their noses up scornfully. Wolfgang confidently assured me that even Adolf Hitler, our *Fuehrer*, had Karl May books in his personal library. The bookshops were full of these bestsellers. In his books, there was always this German guy who appeared with his better rifle and know-how, sorting out everyone, particularly the cruel white trappers against the brave red Indians.

Roepke Housekeeping

ROEPKE MEALS WERE formal affairs, always on time, with everybody gathered around after their hands had been washed. We always had to be properly dressed. Lutheran Grace would be said attentively before any food could be touched. The grown-ups would do all the talking. For us children, it was a matter of being seen and not heard, eating everything on the plate before us. No coughing at the table under the watchful eyes and ears of the lung surgeon, Grosspapa Roepke. He might whisk you away for an x-ray at his hospital.

Once I had a coughing spasm. At the end of the meal, Grosspapa told me to report to Sister Vera the next morning for a chest x-ray. This gigantic roentgen apparatus in its own separate hall was awesome. As to the results, nobody said anything to me. I really did not want to know about it anyway, recalling all the doctor troubles over my left foot in Austria.

Occasionally, the older sons, Heinz and Juergen, would drop in for a short visit, usually on a Thursday when their dad would be at his private practice in Kassel, or on a Saturday when Grosspapa had his regular beer round with the Melsungen notables.

Otto and Wolfgang, the two youngest ones, were happy-go-lucky types. While Dad was away in town, they would take their chances to raid their dad's precious wine cellar and liven things up in the house. Grossmama, of course, would see to it that everything was put in order again before always-punctual Dad came home.

Juergen would die in 1937 of an infection, leaving behind his young, pregnant wife, Aunt Putti, to give birth to their son, Claus-Juergen, known as Claus. Sons Otto and Wolfgang perished on the Russian front, reported missing in action, never confirmed. They and their daughter Ilse's husband just vanished, together with all those young men as cannon fodder in the war in Russia.

Soon the German school holidays were over. Father and Mutti were still not ready with Wallbachsmuehle. Rosi and I, always a team together, now had to join the primary school in Melsungen, a one-hour walk downhill, one and a half hours back uphill, with a late lunch at 2:30 pm in the kitchen.

At school, there were no more Austrian slates; instead, there were exercise books with pens and separate books for each subject. The pen had to be dipped into an ink pot. Fountain pens were a novelty for grown-ups only. Rosi and I already had our own Pelikan sets, showing them off at school, a gift from our family friends, the Beindorfs: 'Uncle Kurt' had been Father's wartime best friend in Siberia. We were lost in the school crowd during the breaks. The other kids laughed at our funny Austrian German dialect. Luckily, we knew enough of each subject to hold our own in our separate classroom sessions.

Mutti had also arranged swimming lessons for us after school in the Fulda River baths, where she and her siblings had learned to swim in their youth. With a chest harness on a line held by the swimming master on the footbridge, we had to cross the river using the breaststroke movements that we had to practice beforehand in the shallow water on the side. If we went under while crossing the river, the master would pull us up, shouting at us to use our movements. The flowing water felt icy. At first, we swallowed some as we went under. This went on until the master did not have to pull us up anymore. He then told us to swim across and back by ourselves. Once we managed that, it was a great feeling. Even the water did not feel icy anymore. We had become swimmers.

Hitler's Germany

THERE WAS NOW also an increasingly looming awareness of the Austrian-born leader of Germany, Adolf Hitler, 'der *Fuehrer*', who was laying down his law over all Germans in no uncertain manner. He had proven himself as a German soldier on the Western Front in the First World War and had been awarded the Iron-Cross First Class as a mere private. Now he made Germany overrule all the dictates of the Treaty of Versailles and rearm. With his new 'Third Reich', he would lead it ahead of the First Reich, the Holy Roman Empire of German Nations, and Bismarck's Second Reich. This time, he would secure German superiority for good.

Our father and we kids, as Austrians, were challenged to catch up. Father scored when he was called up after the harvests for a military service test. He was appointed a captain in

Figure 16 - German Wehrmacht Captain Otto Von Schweitzer (1937)

the German Reserve Army in 1936, a great promotion from ensign in the Austrian cavalry in 1914 during the First World War.

Wallbachsmuehle Farm, 1936-39

BY OCTOBER 1936, we were in our new family farm, Wallbachsmue-hle (Wall-Stream Mill). There was no actual mill, but the wall-stream came straight down past the north side of the rambling east-facing timbered farmhouse, providing our domestic water. The main stream of the north-south valley was the trout-rich Esse, which also drove the water wheel of our private electricity generator. We were part of the village of Retterode on the southern tip of the district of Witzenhausen, 30km further north from us. Schnellerode, two kms to the south, was the north-east tip of the Melsungen district, with the town another 25km down the road. As the locals would say, we were 'where foxes say goodnight to one another' in the middle of nowhere.

All the hills were state-managed forests full of wild game. Foxes were at the chicken compound at night. Varieties of deer and wild boar in the forest came out to feed in the dark on the farm fields rather than forage in the forest area. Fences could not hold them off. It was not just what the animals ate in terms of the barley, rye, or corn; even worse was what they trampled down while roving around.

Dad had a hunting license for the farm area but had to account to the state foresters for what he shot. Only old and inferior specimens were free to be shot. If his kills were young and promising, he would risk losing his license. When shooting in the dark of the night, it was difficult to judge what kind of animal was being aimed at.

Dad had a try with a high-breed hunting dog, but he and the animal never came to a mutual understanding. Any animal shot and fallen on the farm area would be our property. After spending hours of nightly hunting, the family would then have to eat warmed-up deer meat for weeks. Domestic freezers and refrigerators did not yet exist in rural Europe.

Apart from the rough and wet climate of Hessen, this new primitive farm life was nevertheless exciting for us children. There was so much to see and do with hands-on farm work, and among the streams and rocks and their hidden treasures and animals. All grown-ups slept on Sunday afternoons. I would then round up the local village boys for expeditions into the woods. Often, we would only get back after dark and get told off.

Once I found a shortcut to the Melsungen lung sanitorium. By that time, Mutti's parents had already retired to Wiesbaden, but we five boys knocked on the door of Grosspapa's successor at afternoon teatime and were treated to tea and cake. When we got home in the dark at 10 pm, we found our respective parents frantic.

One of my pastimes would become stalking wild beasts on the edge of the forest when they came over at dusk. Dad would go out to shoot or shoo them off at dawn. I would also stalk and shoot rats around the pigsty with my air gun. Dad would pay me one mark for every kill I delivered to him.

Two novelties were a telephone and the newly built house extension block. The telephone was on a high shelf in the main entrance hall so that children should not reach it. Heating using an extension from the big kitchen stove was only available on the ground floor. Elsewhere we had risky oil lamps and candles that had to be used, which we children were not allowed to handle by ourselves.

The extension was a new, square connected building, a salon that held the big Gneixendorf pictures and furniture, and a library with all the books around a stylish reception area. This extension came alive only when we had visitors. For me, it proved an easy escape from the scramble in the main house to hunt for interesting things to read. Ulla Mutti always had an open door for visitors to enliven this annex, but we were a long way off the beaten track for quick, casual visitors.

Altogether it was a wild place. We kids had to clean our boots every time we came home. They had to be taken off on the steps, cleaned, and left in the front lobby. Everybody had to be up at six in the morning. Once every weekday, a red post office van would come past, splashing puddles over our front doorsteps. In the summer, it became a cloud of dust against the windows. The truck would only stop if it had mail for us.

Saturday mornings found everybody sweeping and cleaning the house inside and out. Mutti and the village wives would bake the traditional fruit flan cakes for Sunday. Saturday night was bath night. Everyone took their turn to bathe in a sit-in metal tub in the kitchen, using water heated in an enormous pot on the kitchen range. No churchgoing for us on Sundays in this Lutheran heartland.

All this led up to a standing rule: school homework had to be completed before sunset. After that was the communal dinner around the big table, followed by board and card games until the kids' bedtime at 8 pm. This became a family tradition, which our parents kept up into their old age. We three big ones slept in a space at the top of the house under the roof in bunks that Dad had built for us.

Uncle Georg soon arrived to bring Grandmother Lilli, our 'Mamah', and our Aunt Tilla from Austria. Mamah and Tilla had their own suite of rooms on the north side. Mamah was doing poorly when she arrived and died soon after they had moved in. We children were kept away from the funeral.

Farming had become fashionable in Germany with Hitler's pledge for national self-sufficiency. People wore traditional folk costumes, and even 'townies' were celebrating the spring and harvest festivals. Mutti enjoyed doing it all. She had even installed an outside baking oven to bake our own healthy ryebread. She baked enough of the big, round loaves to last three weeks, meaning that a new baking was a festival day for us with fresh bread. Dad always ate white bread from the village shop because of problems caused by his Siberian war years.

Peter was still Mutti's three-year-old cry-baby who did not play much with us, the biggies. By 1937, he had been joined by two new babies, sister Brigitte (Gittli) and nephew Claus-Juergen Roepke, the son of Mutti's younger brother, Dr. Juergen Roepke, who had died in the army after a botched-up appendix operation just before Claus was born. His bereaved wife, nurse Aunt Putti, could no longer manage him on her own. Finally, our dark-haired sister Heidi joined us in November 1938 at the Kassel Hospital. We were lucky to have Grosspapa's black Adler limousine for Dad to take her to the distant Kassel Hospital in time.

Figure 17 - Ulla -Mutti and Children Wahlbachsmeuhle (Circa 1938)

High School in Lichtenau, 1936-1940

MY FIRST REAL challenge came after our move to Wahlbachsmeuhle in 1936. At age 10, I now had to start high school, and I was due to join the *Jungvolk* wing of the Hitler Youth. The only close high school was in the town of Lichtenau, four km up the road from Wallbachsmuehle. The Lichtenau private high school was an affiliated high school. Parents of the region had clubbed together to found it, so that at least there could be a high school education for eligible 10- to 14-year-old scholars of the area. The classes were small, and the teaching was expected to be up to city standards. The teachers were young and soon moved on. With a good memory, I had never needed to take school learning seriously to get good passing marks.

Compulsory schooling ended at the age of 14. Virtually all kids over 14 were then job training apprenticeships took the place of their education. They were also obliged to become members of the Hitler Youth, the *Jungvolk*, and the Hitler Girls, the Bund Deutscher Mädel (BDM); their weekly meetings would be in the evenings after work. For those of us who continued on to high school, our meetings, on the other hand, were on Saturday mornings when there was no school. By 1936, membership in these youth groups was made mandatory for all kids from their 10th birthday.

The Emperor's New Clothes

IN AUSTRIA, WE children had grown up with the tales of Scandinavian authors such as Selma Lagerlof and Hans Andersen. We had got to know them well, read to us by Mamah. Now our Lichtenau headmaster had picked a three-act play version of Andersen's *The Emperor's New Clothes* as the high school show for the Lichtenau social scene. In its expanded version, the play had two swindler tailors rather than just one, selling the vain emperor purely imaginary suits. Dr. Schelhoes picked Willy Schalles and me for these two leading roles. He personally directed the show.

Willy was good at anything he took on, always the top of the class and winning national prizes with amazing Meccano constructions. But I, the shy outsider, was always awkward in public. What made Dr. Schelhoes pick me, likely to lose the thread mid-play? And yet, it was such a great challenge, if only I could rise to the occasion. I worked hard at it. Willy and I became a cheeky team. The final applause in the packed theatre was overwhelming. Dad, Mutti, and Tilla were dumbfounded. Sister Rosi was actually proud of her brother for a change.

Willy would later end the war as a German prisoner of war in the USA. He then came back to Lichtenau, following his father as a manager in the local sailcloth factory until his retirement at age 65. We had only one post-war phone conversation.

Jungvolk Service

I WAS THE only boy from our nearby village, Retterode, to go to high school. The regional leaders of the *Jungvolk* were senior high school boys from Lichtenau, who were enrolled at the state high school in the city of Kassel, 25 km away by train from Lichtenau. They made me the chosen leader of the Retterode *Jungvolk*, which consisted of 16 boys, aged 10 to 13. This fortuitous break was perhaps because my parents had a telephone. Sister Rosi also became the Retterode girls' leader in 1937 when she joined me at the high school in Lichtenau at age 10.

From our parents, I got a bicycle for my 10th birthday. This was essential for high school, *Jungvolk*, and just getting around quickly since there were no buses. Father would get out our big Adler car only for special trips such as going to Kassel. My bicycle meant also welcome freedom from home chores.

None of us had any prior *Jungvolk* experience. The top priorities were to get uniforms from a shop in Lichtenau, collect obligatory membership fees, and get everybody to the Saturday morning parades. Ideology was not our concern or interest. That was dished out by the adults and taken for granted by us. Any of us repeating all this official stuff was a bore.

Year 1936 was the year of the Berlin Olympics. Hitler's Germany made it a prestige object to show the superiority of German fitness to the world. Athletics and team sports had been especially promoted since 1933, and physical training for all schools was upgraded to main subject status. The effect of this was that suddenly we *Jungvolk* boys had something exciting to do on our Saturday mornings, training and competing in 60 m, 100 m and 1000 m runs, in long and high jumping and all the other athletic tests. The villages had already restored their athletics facilities and playing fields. Along with our team, I became a more competent athlete. It was great beating the Lichtenau boys in contests.

Whenever Heinz or Georg (our local leaders from Lichtenau) came to our Saturday meetings, we were told off, disciplined, and chastised for improper dress and poor attendance in typical military barrack drills. Luckily for us, these leaders had too much on their hands anyway with Lichtenau and the other villages. From 1937, membership fees were abolished. Collecting and banking them had been a real chore for me.

I got closer to Heinz through a friendship with his nephew, Jochen, and to Georg through his younger brother, Willy, my 'tailor-partner' in the school play. Willy was such a high school achiever, and Georg a great sportsman. I really admired them. When Lichtenau opened its swimming pool, Georg swam the whole 33.3 m length underwater in one deep breath. I would try to achieve this all my life from then, with varying success.

I never met Georg again, but in 2000, 64 years later, sister Irmgard and her husband, Horst, took me back in their car to Lichtenau and Retterode. We found Heinz at the family-owned pharmacy block and called on him. He had been crippled during the war in a motorcycle accident in Russia. My friend, his nephew Jochen, did not come back from the Russian front, like Otto, Wolfgang, and so many others. By the end of the war, there were few families who had not lost a father or a son: Grosspapa and Grossmama lost two sons in Russia as well as Juergen, who had died before the war. The grandparents were informed that they were missing in action, but no bodies or personal artifacts were ever returned, nor were their deaths confirmed: by this late stage, Germany was in dire straits.

Adolf Hitler Comes to Kassel

OUR *JUNGVOLK* LEADERS recognized our improving performance by including our village unit in the contingent that was required in Kassel on the streets through which *der Fuehrer* and his entourage of Mercedes cars with dignitaries would travel on this unique occasion, his only official visit to the city. Rumour had it he did not like Kassel, so all the arrangements had to be even more superior and correct: *der Fuehrer* was known to be capable of the most fearful outbursts of fury.

On the appointed Sunday, we were on the early train from Lichtenau to Kassel. When we arrived, we were allocated to a section of the approach road. The Kassel boys had all the central spots. There were a few passing civilians around. Eventually the *Fuehrer* cavalcade approached.

As a long procession of black Mercedes cars passed by us, our *Fuehrer* stood upright next to the driver in the first one in his brown uniform, stony-faced, looking neither left nor right. As the *Fuehrer's* car passed, we stood silently in attention. If we had cheered him, would he have waved back to us? If he did not notice us, we certainly looked at him in awe. The leader of the whole German Reich was passing by a mere three meters in front of us. What greater honour could there be, being briefly so close to him? What a chance to show off about it back home, boasting that we had been face to face with Adolf Hitler in Kassel!

Figure 18 - Jungvolk Leader Helmut

Summer Camps 1937 and 1938

DURING THE FOLLOWING two summers, 1937 and 1938, our parents let me join the exciting *Jungvolk* tent camps organized during the long summer school holidays, reached by means of a special train. None of the village boys were able to join. Their parents needed all hands for the harvesting season or did not want to spend the money. Up to then, I had always been part of our harvesting team like them.

In 1937, we camped in tents on the North Sea island of Langeoog, travelling there by special train from Kassel. From these camps, I came back with a growing repertoire of songs, performance tricks, and boy-scout capabilities and ocean swimming in the North Sea.

In 1938, we camped at a stream near Bad Reichenhall in the Bavarian Alps, in the area of the Berghof. The *Fuehrer* was staying in his Berchtesgaden retreat over the other side of the mountain. So, on a rainy day, we clambered for two hours over the mountain on precarious footpaths to the entrance of the Berghof, eager to meet him. We stood there with a growing crowd of hopeful visitors, waiting for the *Fuehrer* to come out to greet us. The *Fuehrer* did not appear. We were soaked to the skin when we struggled back, disappointed, to our tents.

This *Jungvolk* camp was quite close to what had been the border with Austria until March 13, 1938, when Austria ceased to be a nation and became the German *Ostmark*.

This German reunification, the *Anschluss*, was the first step in the escalation to more aggressive German expansion phases. All the Austrians had to do was to stay put to become German. For us in particular, it meant that we would be directly in touch with our mother's family and relations in Austria again. All were happy and hopeful, except minorities of Austrian patriots, communists, and Jews.

Within our family, there were resisters: Uncle Walter Conrad, as an Austrian diplomat, had been thrown into prison during the war for having opposed the *Anschluss*. On the up after the war in 1946, he became the first post-war Austrian ambassador to the neighbouring Yugoslavia. And then there was Baby Schmidt, the dashing Hungarian Jewess and close family friend near Gneixendorf, who had given Rosi the black doll. She continued her life throughout the war unreported and unharmed as Frau Schmidt.

Summer 1939 in the Sudetenland

OUR GRANDMOTHER'S YOUNGER sister, Aunt Else of Gritta Mutti's family, was married to Uncle Hannes Kluge, the youngest of three brothers, second-generation owners of the large I.A. Kluge linen textile concern, the largest of its kind in Czechoslovakia. Their plants were spread around the foothills of the Riesengebirge (Giant Mountains) in the northern part of the Sudetenland. The Kluges had personal relations far and wide, particularly also with England, Scotland, and Northern Ireland, where all the machinery for their factories had come from.

There were no more *Jungvolk* summer camps. The top senior leaders had been called up for war service. Aunt Else was inviting the wider family to stay with them during the 1939 summer. She also dropped by Wallbachsmuehle at the beginning of our school vacations and offered to take us three 'Gritta children' to this family holiday get-together. All the other Austrian and Sudeten cousins would be there.

Our parents let us go. Dad warned us, 'When they offer you wine, as they will, you must always politely refuse it.' Uncle Hannes personally picked us up in his large Tatra car after an endless train journey. Their large house with gardens and a tennis court on their medium-size farm was already full of family.

Bertha (Bertl), the only daughter of Uncle Hannes and Aunt Else, was 12 years my senior. That summer, she was on vacation from her university studies in Berlin. She had books such as *The Seven Pillars of Wisdom* and *The Revolt of the Masses*. She remembered our parents as newlywed visitors and how she had been captivated by Gritta Mutti's personality and beauty.

She was studying geopolitics with Prof. Haushofer, who, as early as October 1939, had predicted: 'After this war the frontier of Russia and the USA, will be along the river Rhine.' It actually settled along the Elbe River 300 km further east, and finally, the Oder River.

As a friend of Hitler's deputy, Rudolf Hess, Haushofer became a Gestapo suspect when on May 10, 1941, Hess took his solo flight in a Messerschmitt fighter plane to Scotland, desperate to engineer a peace deal with Britain. Haushofer was involved in the underground resistance and was arrested after the 1944 attempt on Hitler's life. He was shot by the Gestapo when the Russians closed in on Berlin in 1945. Indirectly, I had become one of his students when I moved in with the Kluge family in 1941, and Bertl shared her course papers and journals with her nosy cousin.

This 1939 holiday was a hive of fun family activities. We learned to play tennis and were treated more like adults. Reconnecting with our Austrian and Bohemian cousins was fulfilling. Even more exhilarating was the immersion in our Austrian cultural heritage going back generations. Tennis, gardening, and work on the farm always needed volunteers. In the evenings after dinner, we joined long discussions on the terrace with a glass of wine. We felt we belonged.

The long train journey back to Kassel was our first trip ever travelling on our own. Never again would I travel under adult supervision, except of course on military transports during the next 10 years. Bertl, her parents, and her future children became part of our wider life story.

The Approaching War

THE LATE SUMMER of 1939 would be the last for us in Wall-bachsmeuhle. By August, mutual provocations and incidents on the frontier with Poland had escalated from week to week. Things were coming to a head. Everybody was apprehensive. Armies were concentrating on both sides of the frontier.

On Friday, 1ST September 1939, the motorized German forces broke into Poland. It was all over within three weeks. Hitler had pre-empted the fate of Poland by an improvised nonaggression treaty with Soviet Russia in August 1939. Germany occupied west and central Poland to the Bug River. Soviet Russia muscled in and regained much of the territories it had lost after the collapse of the Russian empire in 1918, including eastern Poland, Lithuania, Latvia, Estonia, and Bessarabia. The Russian attempt to regain Finland failed due to the stubborn resistance of the Finnish army under Marshall Mannerheim.

Although England and France could not do much directly to protect Poland, they were treaty-bound to join the war against Germany. We received the news with heavy hearts on Sunday, September 3, 1939.

Early Wartime Mobility

FOLLOWING THE QUICK and successful German invasion of Poland, our farm was overflown by British planes during the nights, dropping leaflets proposing to stop the war. Life seemed to revert to more normal operations. We children had no idea that our parents were actually selling our farm. Father would be called up, and Mutti would not be able to cope on her own with six children and a problematic farm.

Wallbachsmuehle had been really nothing but trouble. We would have to be out by the end of the 1939 harvest.

Now, just before Easter, came the surprise German occupation of the whole of Norway and Denmark as part of the Narwick battle with Britain. On May 10, 1940, the war became even more serious as German forces took neutral Holland and Belgium to enter France from behind its Maginot fortress line. The French had to sign a dictated armistice with Germany on June 22nd and with Italy on June 24th. The British expeditionary forces, pushed back to Dunkirk, just managed to return home.

At the beginning of the 1940 summer school vacation, we boys of the top form in our private high school decided to do a cycling tour to the Rhine and Frankfurt. The war with France was just over. There was uncertainty as to what was permitted or not. Our parents agreed that we could go. We were determined to keep out of the way of any officialdom, particularly the police and party organizations, including the Hitler Youth. This gave us quite a few problems finding isolated farm sheds to stay the night and preparing food in off-road hiding spots.

After a long roundabout trip down the Lahn River and up along the Rhine, we cycled into Wiesbaden. We descended for two nights upon our now retired Roepke grandparents, who put us up in their basement. We inspected Frankfurt, including the old Ghetto and the Cathedral, where I proudly showed my pals the imposing black marble memorial plaque of the Schweitzer family with its gold letters. Extensive bombing would later split this family memorial, to be replaced by a modest, small copy on the north side of the main hall. Our family was not consulted.

After our return home, we boys never met again.

PART 4

GERMAN WARTIME LIFE 1940-1944

All Change: High School
in Wiesbaden 1941-2

FATHER RECEIVED HIS call-up papers and joined the German occupation forces of France in 1940 as a military regional farming controller once our farm was sold. For the last six months of the war, after France had been liberated, he would head a commando policing the roads north of Frankfurt. After the arrival of the US forces in early 1945, he rejoined Mutti after a brief spell as an American POW.

With Father's departure to the front in 1940, Ulla Mutti had needed to find a situation that would tide her over with her children, Peter (8), Gittli (3), and Heidi (2). She took over the management of the Hornsen farm household of Herbert Backe, the then Deputy Minister of Food. He was expected to stay with his family in Berlin and was looking for someone he could trust to look after their farm home. Mutti's stay at Hornsen lasted a year.

Our family was now split up. Sisters Rosi (13) and Irmi (11) joined Aunt Spatzl's family in Wuerbenthal, Sudetenland. I, at 14, was to join the now-retired Roepke grandparents in Wiesbaden to improve my education at a superior city high school there.

I arrived in Wiesbaden in time for the second 1940-41 school term. In my previous private high school in Lichtenau, I had been in the technical (rather than the classical) German high school stream of the gymnasium. My application to the Wiesbaden high school,

initiated on my behalf by Prof. Dr. Onkel Grosspapa Roepke, was to
continue at the same form level as in Lichtenau. The headmaster did
not agree, although my final report had been above average. Standards
were officially uniform countrywide. I would have to undergo special
tests. These tests were demanding, and I was told I had failed them all.

Prof. Dr. Roepke came to the rescue; the headmaster showed
him great respect. He agreed to let me in on trial at the *quinta* level,
provided that Herr Professor would arrange private tuition for me
in all the main subjects. That promised, I was in. Grosspapa never
mentioned private tuition again. I was determined to get through
by myself anyway. The idea of private tuition was abominable to me.
School work became my full-time occupation from then until June
1941, when I received a clean pass to the sixth form level.

Now I was also accredited as a *Jungvolk* first-level leader and allocated a group in the south-eastern working-class part of town. There
were very few kids in the Spa area where Grosspapa and Grossmama's home was located. The fairly minimal *Jungvolk* activities included
weekly door-to-door collections for social causes. The popular rule
was for families to have a one-pot (*Eintopf*) meal on Saturdays, usually
thick soups, and donate the savings for social care purposes. I thought
I might do rather well by collecting in this nearby well-to-do suburb.
I was in for disconcerting experiences. Several times the residents
were clearly upset seeing me in my neat *Jungvolk* uniform as they
opened the door to my knock. They either slammed their door in my
face or threw some coins out in the street before firmly closing their
doors. Puzzled, I asked Grossmama Roepke about this. She suggested
that these people might be Jews afraid of the Nazis. I stopped my
unpopular collecting.

During the Christmas holidays of 1940, I joined Mutti and the little ones at Hornsen with the Backe family. Since they were back from Berlin for the holidays, there was no room for me to stay at the house. I had to sleep in a small guest house in the nearby town.

SS-Obergruppenführer and agricultural Minister Herbert Backe was my first encounter with a really important Nazi. At dinner, we kids at the bottom end of the large table would listen to the great man at the top speaking passionately about the future aspirations of German agriculture after the victorious war. Little did anyone know then that in the following years, this man would develop and implement 'Operation Hunger' following the 1941 invasion of the Soviet Union. The aim of this program was to deliberately starve millions of Slavic and Jewish 'useless eaters', diverting and redirecting Ukrainian foodstuffs away from central and northern Russia for the benefit of the invading army and preparing the land to settle the future population of greater Germany in the area once it was cleared. Due to be tried for war crimes at Nuremberg after the war, Herbert Backe hanged himself in 1947 in prison prior to his trial.

The Wiesbaden school was of a much higher standard than my previous school in Lichtenau. All the younger teachers had been called up to army service. We were taught by teachers of the 'Old School', led by Dr. Wagner and his deputy, Dr. Spatz, our form master. No women teachers were in this boys' high school.

Dr. Spatz taught Latin so well and hard that afterwards I did not have to learn much more to get through my finals in 1944. This meant Latin in his class was my essential test, whether I would pass or fail this year. Merciless Dr Spatz was picking on me relentlessly. His acerbic wit revelled on the country-yokel theme, exemplified by my poorly fitting suits that I had inherited from the two-year-older

Gerhard Beindorf, the son of Father's WWI chum.

Dr. Spatz really challenged me all around. Once in a while, he would talk at length about classical Rome in ardent terms, as if it had been the greatest society in history. I was in awe of him. At the final class meeting in June 1941, he commented on my stamina. I was the happiest kid imaginable upon hearing this compliment!

Sunday morning, June 22, 1941, I was on my way to join our school handball team at the Wiesbaden railway station. We were travelling to Idstein for an inter-school match, which we won. This would be the last engagement of my Wiesbaden school life. On the train, I overheard people saying that Germany was invading Russia.

We learned that the Russian invasion had been set up as yet another surprise lightning war. The German troops were already well on the way towards Leningrad and Moscow in the North, the Volga in the middle, and the Caucasus in the South. People were in awe of the successes of this triumphant German military machine.

Wartime 1941-1944

IN EARLY SUMMER 1941, I arrived at the Backe home in Hornsen to find that Mutti was already planning her resettlement from there and had a role for me to play. Mutti would take the two youngest girls to support the young wife and two small daughters of her younger brother, general practitioner Dr. Heinz Roepke. He had been called up and was stationed as an army doctor in occupied Norway. There was space for everyone on the upper floor of his surgery building in Felsberg, close to Melsungen. I was to take eight-year-old brother Peter for a holiday stay in Austria at the home of Uncle Georg, the Lengenfeld estate in Lower Austria. I loved the idea of going back to Lengenfeld, so near Gneixendorf.

The Mystery of Uncle Georg

UNCLE GEORG, FATHER'S older brother, had taken over the utilization of Lengenfeld after the First World War, although he could not legally own it according to his grandfather's will. This complex situation was the result of another family quarrel over marriage. Our family had come together in and around glamorous Vienna from the middle of the 19th century. In 1850, 18-year-old Georg von Schweitzer, our great grandfather, came from Frankfurt to study engineering for a military career in the Imperial Austrian army. Having achieved that, he married the eligible Ida von Kleyle with her Gneixendorf estate in 1862. Their son, Karl (1863-1901), would become our grandfather. Karl became a Doctor of Law in Vienna, in line with the Schweitzer family custom, and took up a civil service career until his engagement to Countess Lilly Wrangel, our grandmother, in 1889.

True to the Schweitzer tradition of father-son opposition, grand-father Karl's father, great grandfather Georg, was outraged at his son's choice. He shouted, 'Impossible, she is a Swedish Lutheran, the parents are divorced, she comes without a fortune'. When Karl insisted, with his mother's help, Georg bought himself the nearby Schloss Lengenfeld and moved out of Gneixendorf.

Georg then made a testamentary treaty excluding son Karl and his children from ever owning the estate. Ownership, as distinct from usage, would pass directly to his eldest great-grandson at age 21. This was the estate where my own Uncle Georg resided. At that time in

1947, I was a German prisoner-of-war camp leader in London. I never knew anything about all this until 10 years later when the question of this left-over vineyard in Austria cropped up. According to the treaty, Dad needed my signature to get the vineyard sold in the mid-1950s. I had no idea that, as the only Schweitzer son in the direct lineage, I would become the legal heir to the Lengenfeld estate in 1947 at age 21. Only after Uncle Georg had died, as the heir, did I need to approve the sale of the vineyard, all that was left of this vanished estate. It had been worked by tenants until this time. I became dimly aware that Uncle Georg had managed to sell the estate illegally during the war. All the proceeds were automatically invested in German war bonds, just as in the case of the proceeds of our Wallbachsmuehle farm sale. All these bonds were, of course, worthless after the war. The new Germany refunded them in the new D-Mark currency. The new Austria did not. Both brothers had lacked commercial and financial knowhow. Monetary affairs had been taboo topics in their lives. With all these easy German lightning war successes, they had bet on a victorious Germany.

The rest of the Lengenfeld estate had been confiscated after my Uncle Georg, grandfather Karl's eldest son and my father Otto's older brother, had been sentenced to prison for nine years for war crimes. Uncle Georg actually only served four years of this sentence due to illness. This was another topic not talked about in the family. Nobody ever wanted to find out if Uncle Georg might have done anything criminal, which would have been shameful.

This summer of 1941 was the only time in my life that I was close to Uncle Georg. He was and remains an enigma, an aloof intellectual. During the week, he was working in Vienna, but I never discovered what exactly his job entailed. Weekends he would come home to

Lengenfeld. Although he must have been a committed Nazi from very early on, he said nothing about it, and I never saw him in any kind of party uniform. He took me with him on the hunting trail of the estate, and also to Vienna for a week in 1942, where he had an austere apartment. He went to his office in the morning, and I had the day to myself in the city. I do not remember a military presence in Vienna during this visit.

At Lengenfeld during this summer of 1941, Peter and I kept ourselves busy building a wooden bridge across the village stream, which ran through the garden. Once we walked the 5 km across to Gneixendorf. The mansion had been taken over by the German army. The land was being used for a large prisoner-of-war camp complex, first for French and Russian soldiers, and later also for captured US aircrews.

The mystery of Uncle Georg deepened later. In 1953, married and living in London, I was approached in Piccadilly by an unknown gentleman claiming to be a friend of Sir Alexander Korda, the great Jewish movie producer. Would I take a British passport to Uncle Georg and hand it to him in neutral Liechtenstein? he asked. Uncle Georg had just been released from prison in Vienna and was going to live with my father and Mutti in Germany. I was tempted to go until I realized the illegality of it all, and that I would have to take personal responsibility for any consequences, without recourse. I said no. Uncle Georg died a year later. When I told my father about this, hoping he could cast some light on the encounter, he shrugged his shoulders. I have never stopped wondering what this connection between Korda and Uncle Georg in Vienna in the 1920s had been, and why Korda had belatedly tried to help Uncle Georg come to England.

Austrian Again: The Winkelhof

AFTER OUR SOJOURN with Uncle Georg, Peter and I went back to the new family home in Felsberg in August 1941, where Mutti was already well organised in her usual way. I was now packing my bags to the *Winkelhof*, the home of Uncle Hannes in the Sudentenland where we had spent such a happy, carefree holiday in the summer of 1939. It was now a more settled place off the central war stage, where I could pursue my high school studies in nearby Arnau. Aunt Tilla had already been resident there for a year. She would teach me English to catch up with my new form at school, where English was taught from the start.

The Arnau state high school with its boy majority was just three km down the road from the *Winkelhof*. This time, arriving as a 'Wiesbaden city slicker' and a Kluge relation, I was accepted as I came, no questions asked. Somehow, through my various school changes with different form promotion cycles, I had become the youngest form member in Arnau. Most of my new mates were born in 1924 and 1925. I was the only one born in 1926.

Our form collectively joined an evening ballroom dancing course. I was the odd youngster usually without a girl to dance with. I never quite got over the embarrassment, ending up a poor ballroom dancer for the rest of my life.

The next physical challenge for me was skiing. As winter closed in and snow fell, all the youngsters were on their skis. They had been doing it since they were toddlers. I had to catch up from patchy beginnings under our father's direction on the farm in the pre-war years. Before the First World War, Uncle Hannes as a youngster had been one of the early pioneers of skiing in the area. It was then exclusively a gentleman's sport.

Although at age 15 I was now of Hitler Youth age, as a *Jungvolk* leader I had the option to remain with the *Jungvolk* in one of the honorary leadership functions. The senior local area *Jungvolk* leader was one of my new form mates. He reckoned he would be called up to war service within a year. He wanted to hand the position over to me before he was called up.

Frost, ice, and snow of great severity were at this time also challenging the poorly prepared German forces in Russia. Frostbite would account for even more human losses than war wounds, and together, they were a fatal combination. The overextended army supply lines became a nightmare, given the primitive road and rail infrastructure over vast distances. The radio news we received of course played it all down to a 'natural winter pause in preparation for the final blow in the spring'.

In December 1941, Japan's Pearl Harbour attack resulted in the USA declaring war on Japan on December 8th and Hitler declaring war on the USA on December 11, 1941, widening the Euro-Russian confrontations into a worldwide all-out war, now a literally deadly battle between the Allies and the Axis powers.

Everybody had to get used to food and clothing rationing based on the issuance of cards and coupons. Our *Winkelhof* farm could have been a handy source of unofficial plenty for us, but the Kluge family on principle did not want to give in to temptation. This was the rule, apart from occasional lapses. All in all, I would experience food rationing in one form or another for 10 years, from 1940 to 1950.

The Kluges also volunteered to give free board and lodge to wounded German soldiers released from hospital but not yet fit to return to active service, who had no family to stay with during their convalescence. My hopes of learning something about their actual war experiences from them were always frustrated by their unwillingness to talk about it. Soldiers talking about it was also punishable.

Apart from trains and packed-full buses, all travel had to be by bicycle or on foot. There were no paved roads anywhere, except in town centres. There were no petrol allocations for private cars. The big Tatra car was jacked up in the garage to save the tyres.

The lightning wars were over by the end of 1942. Holding the lines was now the problem. Day and night bombing of Germany was increasing. By January 1943, the German Russian front was collapsing, and Rommel's North African forces surrendered. Germany reduced the call-up age to 16 for boys and 17 for girls.

The Turn of the Tide

ONCE A YEAR, there was a conference for all the Sudetenland *Jungvolk* senior leaders in centrally located Prague as a cherished perk. I attended it for the first time at Easter in 1942. Sleeping accommodations were in youth hostels. All the events took place in a classy location and included classical music performances and cultivated lectures. We also had an exclusive theatre performance of a German version of Bernard Shaw's 'Saint Joan' drama. All this was part of the deception and denial, of pretending to be "normal" while at war with England, Russia, and the USA.

I was completely captivated by the contemporary tone and lively argumentative dialogue of the Shaw drama. Everybody knew Schiller's *'Die Jungfrau von Orleans',* (The Maid of Orleans) as the staid, standard German high school fare, but here, Joan's inspired sense of purpose in the tangles of religious and political intrigues and aspirations pointed me towards re-evaluating the Nazi system and my role in it.

Eighty percent of our group was shocked and walked out after the first act. The rest of us were glued to our seats. I went out of the theatre shaken, more alert, critical, and independently minded. I felt personally challenged. True to form, I did not let on to anyone about my mind-changing experience. The reaction of the conference after the walk-out was typical. Nobody talked about it. It was all too controversial. Conforming and discipline were what counted and had to be demonstrated at this stage of the war.

At the start of our 1943-1944 high school year in September 1943, our Arnau form numbers had been reduced from 28 to 10, since all the older boys had been called up for their war service. We were nine girls and one boy, myself, left behind. People on the bus and in the street would ask me what was wrong with me. I looked healthy. Why was I not at the front?

During my waiting time for the home bus after college, I would wander across to the office of my professional Hitler Youth district commander, Erich, and share a cup of tea with him. He was freed from military service because of his polio-stricken leg, which also hindered him from getting around his district. He told me he had a vacancy for a paid assistant and would take me on as his deputy, as long as my call-up deferment would continue after my final exams. High school attendance in those days was rather exceptional and generally limited to the children of the professional middle classes. Hitler Youth leadership positions were almost automatically given to all-rounder high school boys.

Due to my call-up deferment, I was soon *Stammfuehrer*, leader of approximately one thousand boys from ten years old to call-up age. With the worsening war situation by the end of 1944, the final high school exams were now pulled forward from June to February 1944, but my deferment continued unchanged until the end of July. I was the only fit male in the whole district to take the *Abitur* final exam. As Erich's deputy with a motorised bicycle to get around the district for him, I became part of the official establishment that was under growing pressure to improve its performance in preparation for victory.

Figure 21 - Helmut Hitler Youth in Sudetenland, 1944

Life at the Winkelhof

MY EPIPHANY OVER 'Saint Joan' also fitted in more with the open out-look of the Kluge family and their pre-war international relationships with the Scottish manufacturers of the machinery for their factories. On a visit with Uncle Hannes to one of his factories, I saw Jewish slave labour at work for the first time, evident by the yellow star worn by them in the factory. A girl stared at me; I stopped and stared back.

By the summer, Uncle Hannes had fallen out with his brothers and volunteered for military service at age 57. He served as major in the military transport services, controlling the railway lines south of Naples in 1943. When back on leave, he would openly talk about a chaotic mismanagement of the German forces in the area. It would prepare me for what I came to experience a year later in Latvia and Germany during my call-up, training, and at the front.

Irreverent and negative comments on political issues were part of the normal conversation at the Kluges.

In our own home, critical discussions had always been out of favour. Aunt Tilla took offence at the free-flowing Kluge talk, condemning it in her diaries, which came to light only after her death. She did not dare voice her objections out loud. In these diaries, she contrasts their 'disloyalty' with my own *Jungvolk* activities. Reading these diaries so many decades later, I am amazed that I had never realized Tilla's absolute devotion to Hitler and her faith in him. Some of her entries end with '*Heil Hitler*'.

By now, Bertl had quit her studies in Berlin and took overall charge of the household and farm. The garden had been turned over to growing vegetables for the family. Food was becoming scarce, as was everything else. Irrespective of the war, there was always a coming and going of visitors, including the wounded soldiers on recovery leave.

The most frequent visitor to the *Winkelhof* was Lieutenant Dr. Ernst Brass. Somehow, he managed to drop by every few weeks. Bertl and Ernst would marry in February 1944. I felt quite jealous, as she had become my special family friend.

According to his children, law student leader Ernst had been arrested when Germany occupied Czechoslovakia in 1939 and imprisoned by the Gestapo. He was released on the condition that he join them.

At the end of the war, Ernst went back to Prague, but due to his Gestapo associations, he found himself there as a designated 'traitor'. He could only save his life by pretending to be his younger brother and fleeing to his mother's beautiful family estate near Lindau at Lake Konstanz.

With the Russian advance in early 1945, Bertl and her baby boy were now in serious danger. Ernst had arranged a Special Services truck for them to be taken to Bavaria. On arrival in what was by then US-occupied Bavaria, the Americans arrested her as a war criminal suspect and took her child from her. As a war criminal suspect, Bertl found herself in the company of the wives and relations of the top Nazis. She spent two years in this war criminal camp. With her fluent English, she soon became a spokesperson for these women. When I met Ernst again in Lindau in 1957, the once-charming talker had become a reclusive alcoholic.

Waiting for Call-Up

EARLY IN 1943, I had been officially notified that my army call-up would be deferred due to my age, allowing me to finish high school. In 1944, an elite, motorized Waffen-SS band arrived in the village playing cheery tunes to a gathering crowd. They wanted volunteers. The Waffen-SS was Himmler's rival volunteer counter army, created in 1940 to show the stolid *Wehrmacht* how idealists win wars and to compete for daring assignments to prove their worth. All this had to be achieved in a hurry to make their mark. Rumour had it that they were accident-prone, which meant excessive casualties. There was always something sinister about Himmler with his security services.

Chatting to the band members, they told me about the camaraderie among all the ranks and their sense of purpose, without the tedious parades and drills of the regular army. Yes, I could choose which branch I wanted to join. Yes, I could join the armoured reconnaissance tank regiment. My deferred call-up? No problem. We are in charge. I signed up: it seemed to be worth a try.

Dad looked aghast. By the time I was eventually called up by them to Riga in July 1944, they were turning into a callous pretence. To say so became a growing deadly personal risk.

Hitler Youth Adventures, 1944

I REPRESENTED HITLER Youth leader Erich at functions and funerals, and organised tent camps during school holidays and local athletic competitions at weekends whenever possible. By chance, I found among Erich's files a policy prospect for a youth leader fitness gold medal. This decathlon of 10 different demanding athletic tests had to be passed by youth leaders from a minimum age of 18 at three-year intervals to re-earn and retain the gold medal. Erich admitted he was authorised to judge such tests. He was prepared to run a test if I could produce at least five candidates. Sure, I would do that, but what about the minimum age of 18? Erich promised to get official exemptions for us youngsters.

Six of us did the tests under Erich's supervision over several weekends. Waving his walking stick at us, Erich was a relentless driver and judge. In due course, he later handed me my gold sports medal number 14515, the only medal I ever received in my life.

Some weeks later, during the big yearly Hitler Youth summer camp under Erich's management in 1944 at the Adelsbach rocks, a couple of

Figure 22 - Helmut's Sport Medal (1944)

us wanted to liven things up. We decided to race through the camp at night masquerading as escaped British air-force men, yelling wildly in English. Our effect was devastating. The kids went berserk and grabbed whatever weapon they could to use against the 'enemy'. Of course, we promptly slipped into the camp again, back to our normal selves. When we told Erich, he was completely shattered. He could not get over the shock that our escapade had caused. He was shaking and kept saying: 'Never again, never again'. We two were ashamed of our foolhardiness, but at the end, the campers said to us it was the best camp they had ever been to. Eric kept silent about it.

Call-Up: Training Camp

I GOT MY call-up papers to report to Riga, Latvia, on the July 20, 1944, the day Colonel Stauffenberg had tried to assassinate Hitler. The whole German system went into a spasm of chasing and killing renegades. I would have to be exceedingly careful. We volunteers turned out to be the last set of available recruits. We were retained for the nominal continuation of behind-the-front-line Waffen-SS training establishments for infantry courses in six-week cycles.

En route to Riga, I stopped in at Felsberg to say goodbye to the family. I was doing my duty. That night, a barrage of heavy British bombing raids passed over on their way to Kassel, 30 km away. Dressed in my best Sunday suit, I journeyed via Berlin, Koenigsberg, and Memel for the better part of three night journeys. We happened to have been on the last German train that

Figure 23 - Off to War

reached Riga before the Russians cut the connection.

Riga station was a black hole from a bomb blast. We found part of our unit nearby and slept on the floor of some beach chalets, waiting for orders. We were called in to load and unload crates and pack materials. Eventually we were a group of about 120 recruits not kitted out. We were piled into a holiday steamer to sail on to Gdansk at night for fear of submarines. On a slow train through West Prussia, we landed in an improvised tent camp in Angermunde for six weeks in a tent camp, waiting to be supplied with our kits.

By the end of September, we were on a train again to Paderborn in Westphalia. Finally, our six-week basic war training course took place there, less than 100 km away from Felsberg, which I had left in July at the start of these two months of shuttling around. My Sunday best suit was now in rags. During these two months, I had never encountered a Waffen-SS officer: we were dragooned by frustrated, irritable sergeant and corporal types.

One of the inspiring stories of the First World War for me was how British and German soldiers on the Western front in France had spontaneously climbed out of their trenches in 1917 and celebrated Christmas together in their no-man's land. As a soldier waiting for assignment to the front, I was wondering how our ragbag lot would rise to the occasion in 1944. It was unspoken but obvious to all that this would be the last Christmas of this war.

On the road, we marched 10 km with our backpacks to the Waffen-SS Staumuehle camp in the Sennelager military training complex. There we were detailed to wooden huts with triple bed bunks along the walls and a wood-burning stove in the middle. Watery soups and black bread were our rations.

We at Staumuehle were also quarantined after an outbreak of

typhus in the region. The nearest 'mock-enemy' were the Russians in a close-by Russian prisoner-of-war camp. They were detailed out to work on local farms. We did camp guard duties. Occasionally we marched out into the region in full dress uniform formation to fire salvoes of honour at the burial of dignitaries or officers. Most of these military funerals were for victims of the ever-increasing air raids.

Goebbels had just ordered the 16-hour working day for all on behalf of the *Fuehrer*. We were woken by whistle-blowing NCOs at 5:30 am. By 6 am, we had to be washed and dressed on parade and inspection. Latecomers and dress delinquents were punished and had to do push-ups or toilet cleaning. After queuing for breakfast hand-outs, parades for PT exercises, rifle maintenance or kit inspections, all were associated with the usual punishment routines. This is how the NCOs asserted their authority. The only means for us soldiers to avoid being picked on was to do our best and avoid attracting their attention. Over time, it would all lead to settled routines of the typical culprits and those left alone, whose performance would be taken for granted. There were also other ways of easing hardship, such as personal contacts and bargaining.

As one of the rare high-school graduates, I started as an obvious 'clever-dick' target to be picked on and put down. Our daily field training was soon expected to lead us to the edge of the training grounds to farmland, where we could dig up potatoes and turnips for food. On the first occasion, I had to show our lost leader the way back to the camp. I was never picked on again.

We were supposed to belong to a tank regiment. We learned to shoot a tank gun only once. It was mounted on a tank-shaped wheeled chassis; we had to push it to the designated shooting range and back again. Each of us had his chance to quickly load and fire this gun.

The whole operation took a full day. Much more time and effort were devoted to machine-gun training with the amazing new MG 42. Here again, to be effective in the field, it would need at least three people for cross-country transport and use as well as an ammunition supply line. Of course, we never had the opportunity to see and use them in serious action on the front.

At the end of the working day, or secretly before, the stove in the hut had to be lit and the stolen potatoes and turnips from the surrounding farms prepared in one of the metal wash basins. The food would then be cooked in the basin on top of the stove, ready to be eaten some time before midnight. Each hut had its own team of operators and scroungers. The off-duty leaders stayed out of the way in their quarters up the road after 10 pm.

More and more time was spent at night in the supposedly protective open ditches under the trees outside. During the air alarms, rows and rows of British bombers would pass eastwards over us to dump their loads on the big cities. We had to sit it out until their return, empty, two hours later, before the "all-clear" sirens were sounded. My top-bunk position made it possible for me to stay undetected in bed during alarms, but this was risking being reported as missing outside in the ditches.

Our more varied guard duties by now relieved us and our leaders from the compulsive training routines all the time. We found time for ourselves and in person-to-person relationships with our leaders. Ignoring all the formal anti-religiosity of the Waffen-SS, we all felt a need for relief and celebration for the upcoming holidays. Christmas preparations became a common cause for all. Some made presents; others organized. Anything now seemed possible. We came up with an idea: what about a satirical broadsheet in the *Bierzeitung* tradition of the universities, making fun of everything and everybody in verses and drawings?

We took up our shot at press freedom and got away with it. Everybody from our mostly absent commanding officer to the last recruit was profiled and critically versified. We all ridiculed ourselves and, by implication, our overall helpless impossible situation of un-admitted disaster.

Our quartermaster sergeant's typewriter and paper store became the essential editorial base centre for the contributions. Even the printing process on duplicators in a regional office was finessed.

The cover of the final product depicted the steel-helmeted head of a Waffen-SS soldier. Maybe this was why the copy I posted home to my Aunt Tilla, who was the family keeper of news, letters, and memories, and its best correspondent, was not censored by the military mail control. I have retained this broadsheet, probably the sole copy still in existence.

In those days, pretending normal continuity had become the least fatal way forward. Pretending was all you seemed to do. Our commanding officers were not risking their necks anymore. Creeping paralysis was becoming the norm for survival.

On New Year's Day, 1945, we were ordered to repeat the basic military training course after the typhus quarantine was lifted. There was no prospect anymore of new voluntary recruits to keep the set-up going: we were the last. This enabled the camp leaders to continue without disbanding and going into battle. Our second course was carried out in a much more considerate and collaborative way than the first one. In hindsight, this extension in time might have saved our lives, judging from the high casualty rates on the fronts.

PART 5

AT THE FRONT, 1945

Off to the Front

ON THE EVENING of March 20, 1945, returning late from my batman assignment, I saw the front-line allocation list up on the notice board. Assignments to the front had been expected for the last few weeks. You could put your name down for where you wanted to be sent. As was to be expected, all had entered their names to go anywhere other than the Russian front. As the last guy, I was on the list for allocation to the Russian front by default. The posting papers said I had to report to my combat unit forthwith at Dumbrow. The next morning, I collected my papers to a destination in Pomerania, well within the German borders, but by then quite possibly already overrun by the Russian advance.

Regardless of destination, I had to start the journey. This meant I had to be at Paderborn rail station at dusk when the trains would start running.

During the day, rail traffic was paralyzed, risking air raids. My general direction would be eastwards. The passenger train full of service personnel in their different uniforms was on its way past Kassel. I had fallen asleep in my corner seat when suddenly, at about one in the morning, there was a great deal of light and shouting. Our train stopped in the glare light of a British 'Christmas tree' flare. 'Get out- get out!' was the cry. Everybody jumped out and clambered up the embankment. By then, the bomber, having planted the flare, was already returning, firing all guns at the train, and then came back around for another bout before the light of the flare had gone out. A few dead bodies were collected by the railway men and put on the tender before we continued to the next station. Some physical damage notwithstanding, the train continued: all this had become commonplace by then.

There and at every other arrival station, one had to report to the station control officer, where we were given tickets for standard food rations and the next night of the journey. The aim was always for the station commander to get you out and onto the next train the following evening to continue the journey, regardless. Nobody had any idea where my reporting destination might be. This was the travel routine over the next seven days. As my destination was so obscure, I was never on a direct train, but I never experienced another air bombing raid.

On day eight, I arrived in Angermuende and was told that my front-line unit was in the school of the nearby village of Felchow, where I was dropped off. I had come full circle: we were now less than 90 km from where I had left for the Riga call-up two months earlier.

I became the latest addition to a Waffen-SS Tank Squad. It was difficult to imagine that this was part of a tank regiment. It had come down to foot soldiering, which in effect ruled out even machine guns as too cumbersome and weighty with all the required ammunition, even if they could be found.

At the 6 pm evening parade, the corpulent sergeant major took brief note of my details and allocated me to the tail end of the formation. The squadron was made up of three 30-men platoons and a remainder fourth platoon. The commander and the ranked personnel stayed with families in the village. Because it was a rest camp, duty was reduced to 12 hours, from 6 AM to 6 PM.

Apart from the school toilets, there were no ablution facilities. A mobile field kitchen was parked next to the utility shed. The whole school area was fenced in and guarded. A remnant company of about 100 men had just arrived there for a respite after serious combat in Pomerania on the eastern side of the Oder River.

All school furniture had been cleared out and the wooden floor covered with sheaves of straw. This was the resting space for us, like sardines in a can. Once the evening parade was over and the leaders had gone to their private quarters, a radio was always turned on full blast in the hall tuned to the strictly forbidden USA program *Soldatensender West*. It would only be turned off at wake-up time in the morning. For one thing, the music was better than German fare; for another, their propaganda clash with the propaganda of the German radio stations was interesting. The possibility of truth might be somewhere in between. Thus, we had two versions of war and world news, with the *Lilly Marlene* song and all the others as our lullabies.

A Soldier's Life

ALL THE MEN wanted was to be left in peace. All the commander wanted was to chase us around from one parade to another to keep us on our toes. The non-commissioned leaders suggested practice exercises in the nearby woods instead. So, on Good Friday afternoon, we smartly marched out to the woods, singing loudly enough for the commander to hear in his quarters. As soon as we were out of sight, we relaxed into casual walking in the nearby state forest.

One of the corporals wanted a smoke, which I could provide for him from my pocket in exchange for bread. He said with Easter coming, there should really be some better food provided for a change. I told him that would only happen if we did something about it. He then pulled out a handful of live rifle cartridges for me. This was the first time I had live ammunition in my rifle.

We wandered through the woods, the bulk of the men in a large group, chatting away. I shadowed them at a distance, hoping to see some deer they might stir up. Suddenly, I saw a big female deer some 50 m before me. Hesitating for only a moment, I pulled out my gun and fired. The deer fell on the spot. I waited. All the chatting had stopped. Everybody rushed up. I stood back. Those in the know wasted no time cutting up the massive animal, hiding the parts in the bushes ready to smuggle the pieces back to the school kitchen after dark.

Only too aware that I had committed a highly punishable crime, I did not want to draw any attention to myself: no hunting license, trespassing, shooting a deer cow, and stealing state property, among other things. Guilty if found out. On Easter Sunday, I collected my portion of game meat for dinner like everybody else. Our leaders in their private quarters never heard about it, or they looked the other way.

Real War, 1945

ON APRIL 12th, I woke up at night to hear a different tone of voice on the radio, with the announcement that US President Roosevelt had died. The next morning, trucks arrived to take us into combat. Squeezed onto four lorries, we were taken down to the main road in the river valley of the Oder, some 60 km northeast of Berlin. The approach to the river was under heavy Russian artillery fire, creating a great deal of smoke around the riverbank.

Leaving our backpacks on the squadron truck, we found an entire array of guns and ammunition lined up to choose from. Among them were shiny, new, fast precision handguns. They surely must have been what Uncle Heinrich Wimmersperg, my father's dear friend, had developed for the army. They looked professional.

I was seriously wondering whether to ditch my ancient rifle, which was date-engraved 1914. One of the old hands saw me. 'These new designs are too precision smart and will jam with the first bit of dirt', he said, then added, 'The safest are the Russian handguns. They never let you down. They look shoddy, but you can drop them in the mud, and they will still fire when you pull the trigger'. There could be nothing worse in combat than a jammed gun, so I stuck to my faithful WWI army rifle, which had been such a boon in all those weapon parades. For 30 years, it must have been polished by army soldiers before it had been dumped on the upstart Waffen-SS. Now I only needed to dust it off to pass inspections. It was not great at distant target shooting, but it never jammed in all the dirt on the Russian front during the forthcoming days.

In the Thick of Front-Line Combat

HEAVILY LOADED WITH ammunition, spades, bayonets, with steel helmets on our heads, we marched in platoon formation towards the great noise at the river. The meadows were covered by heavy Russian artillery fire in an almighty roar of howling and explosions. Just as we reached the range limit of the Russian artillery firing range, there he was, our captain, in his smart officer's coat, remaining standing on a pile, letting us pass on towards the uproar. We marched past him without any saluting. We would not meet him again until seven days later when we were in full retreat, going west.

With artillery hits exploding all around us, I expected we would spread out for safety, but we continued in tight formation along the track through the meadows. Why were we marching into this inferno in close formation as if we were not a big target? I kept my eyes on the old hands ahead of us, ready to duck instantly when they did in case of a direct hit. They would surely sense if and when we would have to dive to the ground. Luckily, we reached the river edge in full formation.

There was no German presence at all at the riverbank when we got there at about midday on Friday, April 13, 1945. We were the first defenders to arrive. The Russians could have crossed over unopposed instead of shelling the area like crazy.

Now we were detailed in strict parade sequence to the spots where we had to dig our fox holes. We needed to cover the coastline from south to north without any support on our unprotected flanks. Our own group was the motley north tail end of the otherwise battle-tried platoons, who were close-knit buddies among themselves. They had quickly dug themselves into fox holes along the high riverbank.

Our ragtag platoon of 20 was headed by the tall, blond Horst, the most junior NCO, a strong young baker from Bremen. Between us, we were assigned to defend a flat island against the Russians, covered by small shrubs on the northern flank, connected to the main shore by a weir. I tried to learn to make sense of the noises in spite of the resonance caused by our steel helmets.

We had to get across by means of a gangplank instead of being posted on top of the riverbank like the others. Our group included a demoted sergeant major, still in his parade uniform, continuously whimpering and shaking from fear. Most of us had never been in battle before. Horst led us across and calmly indicated spots about 10 m apart for each to dig our foxholes. I dug my hole nearest to his at the head of the island near the gangplank.

Under the intense artillery barrage, we very quickly settled in them as best as we could. The steel helmet now became my fox-hole toilet. There was no real safety because of the nearly vertical trajectory of regular mortar bombs with no warning noise. On the first afternoon, a Russian mine came down behind me, and a mortar splinter struck me halfway up my back, just where my hands could not reach. My blood-soaked shirt and the wound remained caked together for the next five days until the company medical orderly bandaged me up.

During daylight, there was sniping from both sides. There was no sign of any German artillery presence until 6 pm at dusk, when a battery from the west rising behind us opened fire on the Russians with 10 salvoes, exactly at the same time every day. The Russian artillery barrage would intensify towards midnight and reach a growing crescendo from night to night, coming to a complete stop at 2:30 am. The Russians would then attempt to come across with flotillas of floats and boats that multiplied from one night to the next. Our protruding island down-river ended up as the default attempt to land. For four nights, the Russians were eventually driven back, but each night it became less likely. We had no ground support at any time. None of the senior NCOs from the land side ever came across to us.

It also had become obvious that there were no forthcoming supplies of food, drink, or ammunition. Sunday's sandwich packets and filled water bottles had been empty since Monday. We had to be more careful with what ammunition we had left. We were stuck, hungry, and thirsty in our damp holes. Covered in lice and insects, we were still there, anxiously facing the next onslaught.

Horst went back one night for one of those newfangled *Panzerfaust*, German anti-tank rockets. He was sure that sooner or later, the Russians would attack with amphibious tanks. Nobody else wanted to believe this.

On the sixth night, at 2:30 am, the attacking fleet covered nearly the whole river, and we heard the noise of an engine. An amphibious tank was on its way to our island. Horst told us to hold our firing until the Soviets were actually landing. I saw him loading the *Panzerfaust* on his right shoulder as this tank was approaching. His rocket hit the tank directly with a flash; the tank stopped and slowly sank.

The Soviets were moving in on us from all sides, and we fired our rifles on anything that moved in the bushes. Before long, the Soviet artillery started up again with their barrage for the next round. Some Russians had landed on our island. Suddenly it was all over and quiet. They had gone. Now we heard terrible groaning from Horst's foxhole. I crept across and saw that he was slumped down. The back-blast of his rocket must have caught him, and his whole back was bare, burned right down to the bone. He was dying in great pain, He asked me to shoot him. I held his hand and he died. We felt helpless. He had sacrificed his life for us.

At dawn, I discovered a dead Russian soldier just three meters from my foxhole. He had a crust of bread in his forage bag. For me, it was the first bit of food in more than four days.

We were relieved by a *Volkssturm* company of grandfathers and grandsons in the evening. By then, we had been nearly six days without any support, no food or ammunition. We had to leave poor Horst behind in his foxhole grave. We could not have carried him across the plank without attracting Russian attention from across river in the delicate moments of the change-over. Our company would surely not wait for us for a moment under the artillery barrage. We had to run to the spot where we had been unloaded the previous Friday. Everybody there had already finished eating. The field kitchen was about to leave. Nobody mentioned Horst again, the only hero I had met in my time as a German soldier.

Retreat

BY MIDNIGHT, WE were redistributed over four newly dug defensive bunkers about 100 m behind the road along the Oder River. We could now sleep lying down.

I awoke at dawn. Looking through the gun slot, I could see a column of Russian soldiers moving along the edge of the main road. I ran, calling into each bunker, 'The Russians are here! Collect up at the artillery position — Follow me!' All were up in no time and followed me. Up there, the artillery was gone already. We lined up in the usual parade order.

With the least at stake to lose, I was picked as a messenger to go ahead and find the captain and the HQ unit, who might be in the nearest village. I noticed something like rooftops in the distance and headed off in that direction. Halfway along, in the middle of an open field, I was spotted by one of the Russian reconnaissance planes nicknamed 'sewing machines' because of their noise, which could slow their flight. It homed in on me, firing its guns. Hits around me were digging up the ground. It came around again. I kept walking upright to minimize the target area. It worked. The plane moved on.

The village looked deserted. Maybe they had fled already? At the centre under a tree, I saw the squadron truck opposite the village pub. In there, the sergeant-major listened to my verbal report. He would talk to the captain. I turned to find the medical sergeant, who cleaned and bandaged my back wound and bleeding, blistered feet. When the sergeant-major wanted me to report back to the squadron, the medic told him I was wounded and under his care. From then to the end, two weeks later, I became the odd body with the squadron staff to the end of our Waffen-SS existence. There were no more formal parades.

PART 6

PRISONERS OF WAR

An American POW

THE WHOLE SQUADRON came together in crowded Angermuende. Without anyone ordering it, we were all now gathering together to surrender to the British or US forces. The sky was dominated by US and Russian planes, and all public roads were jammed up with civilian and military vehicles, strafed by enemy airplanes during the day.

By Friday, May 4th, we were a growing mass of German ex-soldiers, having surrendered to the American Army, waiting in the wet grassland by the Elbe River. All we had been told was that the US army-controlled pontoon bridge to the west would be open to cross the next morning. Only trucks would be allowed to cross. It was up to us to find a truck driver heading in the direction we wanted to go and to get on before 8 AM.

We looked around for a place to sleep. We were not fenced in, except for the regular farming fences. Having spotted a shed in the distance, a couple of youngsters and I went along, finding that it contained bales of hay. We each lugged a bale next to the truck line and settled on top of them for the night.

Before long, our fine captain, who had stayed behind while we marched forward to the front, accompanied by his *aide-de-camp*, rolled up and demanded hay for their bedding. We wanted to know what they would give us in return. For every armful of hay, they gave us a big bar of chocolate, something we had not tasted for years. We shared the chocolate and slept in comfort until the morning.

The next morning, May 5, 1945, was the date Germany formally surrendered, not that we knew anything about it. 'Go home!' shouted the GI at the barrier to the bridge. Everybody crowded around the growing line of German army trucks for the river crossing. I managed to get on to a truck headed to Eisenach, close enough to where my family lived. We, from the Eisenach truck, became a little community for ourselves.

Nothing but some US army vehicles were on the road. By the afternoon, we were running low on petrol. Some GIs stopped and said we needed to stay at the nearby village overnight anyway because there was an all-night curfew. They would organize petrol in the morning. They commandeered a large farm shed for us to stay for the night.

In the morning, a US army truck arrived for us to get on. We were told it would take us to a station where we would get our release papers. We finally found ourselves in a fenced-in football stadium on the edge of battered Hanover.

May 14th was my 19th birthday. Our truck group prepared a special little birthday party for me, which now became my leaving party, since anybody who had belonged to one of the proscribed organizations, including the Waffen-SS, now had to register separately for screening. The next morning, all of us who were now 'registered suspects' found ourselves on a truck to Staumuehle, which I had left in the middle of March, for my front-line posting.

The Americans had built there a special new high-security compound for us. We were all cooped up, sleeping on the bare floor of the huts, identity parades at 6 am and 6 pm, and all-day compulsory walking along the inside of the perimeter fence. After the 6 pm parade, each hut had to collect US army rations, nominally 110 calories per person, to be shared out by the incumbents. This was always the tensest episode of the day. I was a youngster among grown-ups, who were all nursing their grievances and wanted to be respected according to their ranks. No such luck for them. I was unshaven for months, bandaged, covered in lice and bugs in throw-away clothing, physically the youngest but possibly the fittest.

As we were doing our daily walking, I looked around. Everybody else seemed to trudge around, heads bent down, their feet moving slowly through the thick sand. Then I saw another guy, head up, looking around. Our eyes met. We joined together and started talking. He had been the manager of an IG-Farben chemical plant near Leipzig, and therefore high on the list of suspect perpetrators. He was a lively intellectual in his late thirties. We kept ourselves fresh and alive discussing classical drama in our fraught situation.

Interrogation

DAYS PASSED. ABOUT midnight in July 1945, I was brought from the hut before a young US officer at night, still in my front-line rags. He looked as tired as I was.

'Tell me your story of your life!' he said in fluent German. His natural German made me think he might be one of the Jewish refugees from Germany before the war. How different his life experience must have been from mine.

Every now and then, he would interrupt my summary life story impatiently with sudden questions: 'What do you think of Hitler? Was the war justified? What about the Nazi Party?' I knew the right answers: Hitler? The greatest war criminal; The war? The greatest crime against humanity; The Nazi party? A band of evil fanatics. He nodded his approval.

I was dismissed before I even had finished what little there was to tell of my past. He did not even ask me why I had volunteered for the Waffen-SS.

Surely this was important? Even now, I wonder how I would have answered him had he asked. Whatever I would have said would have been taken by him as either humble truth or blatant whitewash, depending on his overall impression of me. I had taken the easy way out and got away with it. There was nothing heroic about it.

Before the parade the next morning, I was delivered with my backpack to the next compound, which had been the Russian POW camp during my earlier war training but was now the camp for German officers. Structurally it was a decaying raft of vermin-riddled abandoned ex-German army huts, guarded by the Amis, our term for the American soldiers. Under the Geneva Convention, ex-officers had their own superior camps.

Camp Life

THIS CAMP WAS civilised and interesting despite its terrible state. The inmates were family fathers, teachers, and ordinary professionals. They were the kind of soldiers who had been on the home front and in the offices. Their undigested trauma was evident as the talk turned back to the 'good old days' of their youth, before it had all started. There were debating and PT classes, a choir for the good old German folk songs, math, and English classes. There were even good books to read.

I was shocked how my attention span for reading and learning was down to minutes after all these wartime trials. Weeks of reading practice were needed to get me back to a normal range of concentration. I joined the choir and as many of the courses as I could fit in timewise.

For everyone, problem number one was how to get out and home. Nothing else really mattered.

The British Takeover

ALL THIS UNEASY brooding changed once the British Zone of Military Occupation replaced the Americans in Westphalia. The British army treated us as captured soldiers rather than as prison inmates. I found myself the interpreter of a party to collect milk for the camp from the local dairy. The dairy workers plied us with cups of cream while we were loading the milk cans onto the army truck. Back at the camp, I was sick as never before.

We became more aware of what was going on outside. Odd newspapers found their way into the camp and were passed from hand to hand. They were full of stories of German war crimes and those responsible for concentration camp atrocities. No mention of the millions of us locked away as prisoners of war.

The first reaction of us ex-soldiers was righteous disgust at these vile reports. Now everything German was being criminalized. We had never done anything like that. All Germans were presented as subhuman creatures, even worse than the Soviet Russians. Such apparent hatred by the victors stirred animosity towards them as a counter-reaction. What had really happened was not the issue. 'We are in this hell together'. 'We must stick together'. In such a state of protest, anybody who knew better from personal experience or as a participant would be doubly certain to keep quiet about it.

By early September, we were in a totally refurbished clean camp with DDT, hot showers, and completely new outfits. Regardless of previous rank, we were all given ordinary British army garments, except that all outerwear had inset coloured patches to distinguish us from the real Tommies. Nice, but not promising freedom. Before long, we were off on a train from Paderborn to Brussels.

POW Camp In Brussels

BY THE END of September, we were all in an endless tented camp overlooking part of northern Brussels. As far as the eye could see, the camp was neat rows of square British army-issued tents for 10, each on top of a meter-deep dugout. Every 100 tents were wired off separately, and all these compounds were behind a guarded fence system.

We had become part of a gigantic mass of cleaned-up, Tommy-clad POWS still hoping for release, feeling the uncertainty, boredom, and frustration of our situation. The only relief was a controlled postal service for standard POW letters. At long last, prisoners could write POW letters once a month to their families and eventually get news from them by means of our first post-war chance of correspondence with family and friends.

My Austrian Loophole

WANDERING AROUND, I usually ended up at our compound gate where there might be a chance to meet people from the other side and find out what was going on. One day, I got talking to a soldier from the British regimental compound, who told me that the POWs serving there were all Austrians. I quickly impressed on him that I was an English-speaking Austrian. Could I join them and be useful? Two hours later, my backpack and I were on our way to their compound of neat Nissen huts.

The Austrian head of the POWs in the office greeted me like an old friend. His problem? He was short of English speakers. The stores and supplies side had been cornered by a defiant bunch of Poles without an interpreter. Would I go there as their official interpreter?

It was a real challenge. Neither the Poles nor their British keepers wanted anything to do with me. As I lingered, I found out that these Poles had been part of a Waffen-SS commando, likely to be treated as war criminals by the Russians after their release back to Poland. They were desperate and wanted me out of their way. Reporting failure after a week of trying, my new 'friend' thanked me and sent me to the regimental head office instead.

My tasks there were mainly menial, such as keeping the place tidy, managing the lighting, heating, stationery, and office supplies, and being available when required. Much of the day I would spend in my corner, studying the daily set of British newspapers from *The Times* to the *Mirror*.

The only other POW on the premises was Sepp, partner of the mail corporal. He spoke neither English nor French. Friendly and dependable, he had served the whole regimental complex alone until my arrival. Naturally I joined the team. In the dark of the early mornings, we would throw the odd sack of coal to the Belgian farmer adjacent to the regimental office block, which was much appreciated. On some late evenings, we would slip across through the barbed wire to have a drink with him. We were all co-conspirators. The friendly Austrian chefs in the messes would give you a plate of eggs and bacon to eat there and then, out of sight. Anybody wanting stationary items came to me.

My English was becoming more fluent. All these months in an English-speaking environment with newspapers to study were a vital education for me. Through the newspapers, I gained a better worldview, certainly a clear break from the past.

Occasionally I would relieve the corporal operating the regimental switchboard telephone line. Once when the switchboard corporal asked me to take his place while he went on an errand, the colonel wanted a connection and noticed my accent. He publicly gave us a good dressing down in the main office.

From the colonel's desk, I gleaned that the whole camp population would be shipped to England for farm work. From March 1946, the POW transport relocations to England started rolling. By June, the colonel was addressing those of us in the head-office POW compound of the now vacant camp. We really were due to be sent to England, but he would give us a chance to get home by sending us as a sick transport to Germany. Needless to say, this became a detour on our way to England, but a month in transit at the British release camp near Hanover allowed better family communications, including a chat with Dad across the barbed wire fence.

Whenever the POW train to Antwerp slowed or stopped, some guys jumped off. The British army guards did not shoot them. I was staying on course to England.

PART 7

LONDON POW CAMP 1946-1948

Off to Britain

ON A BREEZY morning, we marched to the port of Antwerp and embarked on a British navy minesweeper. The bulk of the guys settled down in the shelter of the improvised bunks installed below deck. I wanted to take in everything and settled before the main mast on deck. As soon as we got into the open sea, our little craft heaved up and down through stiff winds and big waves. This went on until we reached the Thames estuary long after dark. Nearly everybody was seasick, including our armed Tommy guards: nearly everyone, that is, except a few of us. We found ourselves able to roam around freely and help ourselves to food and drink. We never stayed below in the smelly chaos for long.

We docked at Tilbury after midnight. As our bedraggled group climbed off the gangplank, a smiling young Tommy was handing a mug of tea to everybody. He seemed to be my age. I was suddenly overcome by a great impulse of joy, an epiphany, something I had never felt in my life before: England. It still echoes through me every time I come back to England.

Just on the other side of the platform, we stepped into the uphol-stered Pullman coaches of a train and came to rest finally in a neat Nissen hut camp at Bungay, which had been built for the American bomber crews in the war. Nothing happened for weeks. It was now September 1946. We late arrivals seemed to have been forgotten, but then we were taken by train to Liverpool St. Station in London and then trucked to Paddington Station.

There we stood on a busy platform in central London, waiting for the next train. We stood apart, in line with the strict post-war non-fraternizing rulings, when an old railway worker casually walked up to us and started talking to us in English and German. He had been a POW in Germany in the First World War. Our guards and the Bobbies alongside all listened. They were all around on the platform, relaxed and friendly. He waved and cheered us — 'Good luck, chaps' — as we got on the local train to Greenford and a new transit camp.

No. 2 Bomb Disposal Squad-ron Royal Engineers

A WEEK LATER, Major Gibson addressed us in their own Fulham headquarters. I translated. The German bombing raids on England in 1940-41 had left many unexploded bombs buried under the surface. The No. 2 Bomb Disposal Squadron was charged with clearing the greater London area and needed manpower for the job. With us, the bomb disposal manpower for London would double. He wanted us to volunteer for the task and join them.

Did the Geneva Convention sanction prisoner-of-war deployment on such inherently dangerous work? Definitely not. Was the work actually dangerous? Probably not. Major Gibson wanted us to volunteer to bypass the Geneva Convention problem. The older and more senior men among us had reservations about assisting the 'enemy', who had already delayed their return home to their families for more than a year and a half. I reported back to Major Gibson that we were volunteering.

For the rest of this first day, we were clearing up the messy camp site. Somebody had the idea of stacking up the various stray bomb cases as a kind of monument facing the main entrance. The idea caught on, and the monument grew in time to an ever more imposing monument of success.

For some months, we now became part of the London rush-hour traffic into town at 6:30 am. We were now respected as some sort of specialist elite. Everybody joined their working party headed by a sergeant. Each of the 18 teams had their allocated site and the required boring kits, pumps, cranes, and timber to line the vertical shafts towards the estimated location of the bomb. By 5 pm, all teams were expected to have come back to the base.

Each team had its own truck. The Royal Engineers were quite short of qualified drivers. Soon most teams had 'qualified' German drivers. None of these drivers had ever experienced London city traffic, with double tram lines running down the middle of most main thoroughfares. Traffic offenses and damage were initially the order of the day and kept me busy with accident reports and even court appearances.

Every now and then, one of the sites successfully unearthed its bomb, weighing either 250 or 125 kg. The site leader had to report his readiness to the squadron leader, who would set a disarming date, allowing for the police to clear the area of people and allow the press to attend the spectacle. Our major would arrive, climb down the ladder, and unscrew and retrieve the detonator. In fact, no self-respecting team leader would ever have failed to unscrew the detonator beforehand when the bomb had first been laid free. He would then screw it back and report to the squadron leader for the official disarming.

All this became good publicity for the Royal Engineers, but now also for us POWs as well, with pictures and reports in the *Daily Mirror*, *Express*, and *Mail*. Here we were, Germans digging up German bombs. People wanted to get to know us and welcome us back to civilization. All this was reinforced by the Labour government's real measures for German 're-education'.

Figure 24 - Helmut POW leader (London, England)

No. 9 POW Platoon B.D.

JUST BEFORE THE winter, our Hurlingham camp extensions were completed, allowing us to move in with the army unit. Now we had to constitute ourselves as a new POW camp, the no. 9 POW Platoon B.D. According to the Foreign Office, a camp leader had to be elected by the prisoners. Everybody looked at me and said, 'You are already doing it. Get on with it'. A month later, the War Office declared my 'election' invalid. Under the Geneva Convention, a POW camp leader had to be a senior non-commissioned officer. I had been a private. Major Gibson managed to persuade the War Office to make an exception.

Figure 25 - POW Hurlingham Football Team (Helmut front row, second from left)

We had to organize our set-up on British army lines, including our catering, administration, treasury, and first-aid functions. We received the same rations, but our pay was much less, half of it to be a monthly credit to be paid out on release from captivity, the other half paid out in cash for current use. Every now and then, Major Gibson would take me with him on his inspection trips to bomb sites and show me part of the bomb-damaged London on the way.

These were the 'hunger years' in devastated Germany. We were in postal contact with our kin over there. England was also rationed in terms of food and clothing. As prisoners, we were officially allowed to send one parcel of up to 5 lbs a month. Most of us were collecting food and clothes by fair means and foul to send home. The demand for parcels was always greater than the official allocation. Our camp expected us officials to wrangle all the extra parcels past the controls without incident. This was never easy.

Open Camp Life

ONCE ENCAMPED IN Hurlingham, we were free to go out from 5 pm up to 11 pm on holidays and weekends. Although wearing the patch-marked POW uniform was obligatory, certainly at least past the guarded camp gate, most of us youngsters quickly found ourselves civilian supporters outside, and we could change into civilian clothing. If it was a question of staying out overnight or even a whole weekend away, it was necessary for friends to place a bolster that looked like a sleeping body in your bed, so that the guard checking after 11 pm would not be alarmed. During working hours, soldiers and POWs needed a pass from an officer to leave the camp.

I became a member of the Moral Rearmament movement. Once I was invited by an Oxford University student member for a weekend, sleeping at his college, eating out, and going to the theatre. This made a big impression with his fellow students. We were the closest POW camp to both the Foreign Office and the War Office. We became a kind of convenient venue for them to visit and inspect. I got to know Dr. Reichenbach, the Foreign Office Editor of the official POW journal, distributed weekly free to all camps. I wrote socialist articles for the journal, and together we interviewed for the BBC. The Swiss Red Cross sent books and their *Die Weltwoche* magazine. *Weltwoche* became my kind of referee of all post-war reporting. Nobody really wanted to talk about the past. None of our English friends asked awkward questions. Our football team was popular with surrounding amateur clubs, who mostly had no pitch of their own.

For Christmas, we set ourselves a target of getting every POW invited to an English Christmas dinner. It worked. The most interesting engagement for me proved to be the Moral Rearmament movement, also known as the Oxford Group. The Fulham group had the past Fulham mayor as its chairman and Maggie Dobinson as its secretary. On May 14, 1947, they surprised me with a 21st birthday party. Maggie came with her only child, Sheila, my age. Maggie would become my mother-in-law when Sheila and I married in January 1949.

Planning a Future

WITH ALL THE hullabaloo of the bomb-disposal progress, I could not help but worry about my longer-term future. My POW years would count for nothing after my release. In November 1946, I sat for the British Control Commission English Diploma. I got a special mention. Encouraged by this success, I embarked on self-study for the London University matric. My subject choice was aimed to make graduation as easy as possible: English, German, French, Math, and Geography. In Germany, I had graduated in all these subjects except French. I had been taught French for five years in high school before changing to English.

I passed the London matric in January 1948. I had also passed the Wilton Park course in spring 1947. This great honour for a German POW in Britain was meant to enable us to return to the new Germany. I was there as a young nobody among about 30 older, more qualified and experienced associates from the officer POW camps. The demanding lectures in English or German were of the highest order. The lecturers included top politicians such as Jennie Lee MP, wife of Health Minister Bevan. The German language side was provided by eminent pre-war refugees from Germany, such as Professor Mandelbaum. Even if I did not retain much detailed knowledge, this intellectual experience propelled me towards university.

While I was at Wilton Park, the squadron was moved up to Richmond Park. An impromptu public meeting in the evening got me reconfirmed as the camp leader. Richmond Park was open to the public all day long. There were no more barriers or barbed wire. The army camp gate coincided with the Sheen Lane Park gate.

Now Dr. Reichenbach said, 'You should apply to the LSE, the London School of Economics, for a place'. His son had graduated there. He promised to give me his official 'Foreign Office' support. Following my application, the LSE informed me that admission depended on passing a competitive entrance examination. The instructions also stated that I could take this examination on the condition I did not wear prisoner-of-war garb. When on exam day I went to our new major for a pass–out, he

Figure 26 - POW Helmut (Illegally as Civilian)

said, 'One condition: you wear your prisoner-of-war outfit'. I replied: 'Yes Sir', and left the camp to change into civilian dress at the Reichenbach family home.

This written examination took place in an endless exam hall with rows upon rows of British ex-service men and a few girls. What chance could I possibly have to be among the few to get a place? And yet, I got admitted for the 1948 Michaelmas term. This was one more reason for me to strive for a prompt return to London after my release in Germany.

Meanwhile restored Austria had opened an embassy in London. They told me they would issue me with an Austrian passport on the basis of a *Heimatschein*, a certificate of origin issued by the mayor of my hometown. I wrote to the mayor of Gneixendorf and received my certificate by return of post. This could by no means be a foregone conclusion since we had officially emigrated as a family in 1935 and had become German citizens. It was a token of the villagers' bond with our family. All Austrians had automatically become Germans for the seven years that their country ceased to exist from 1938 to 1945 without any paperwork, and then reverted to being Austrians again in 1946.

In all the 10 years I had lived under German jurisdiction, I personally never had any official documentation of German citizenship because I was underage. By the time I registered at the LSE, I was a confirmed Austrian citizen from birth, but still had to get out of being a German prisoner of war. My only legitimation as German would be my British prisoner-of-war release papers, coupled with my German family relations.

All such formalities in those days were overshadowed by the growing indictment of common guilt for the catastrophe and horrific war crimes, elaborated by a world in shock after the event. Exactly what did this guilt mean for all those who were German during those years? Culprits had to be taken to account and punished. Apart from the obvious culprits by their proven deeds, the millions who had more or less willingly been part of this collective criminal folly were now under an obligation to prove in detail that they personally had not done anything wrong. Their future in the new society depended on a successful clearance. Expressing feelings of guilt could only turn them into suspects. Proclaiming innocence was a practical necessity to get on to a normal life.

Was I in my clever move to become Austrian taking advantage of an opportunity which would pay off? Was I not trying to go further by settling in Britain, leaving the guilty sphere altogether for the realm of the rightful accusers? Yes.

Maybe it all depends on outcomes. In a way, our three years as prisoners of war can be claimed as a common punishment for having been involved. Much of it was wasted time just being locked up behind barbed wire. Austria was now thriving. 'Guilty' Germany was working an economic miracle and was stabilizing the European community. I had taken my chances. Maybe we need to ask what we made of them.

My experience and the challenge of London and England were real and meant more to me than a final return to Germany. Keeping close with our family, yes, but Germany as such? Was there anything to do for me there? Did that mean I was a turncoat, a phrase that Hitler had always lambasted as associated with a rootless Jewish scheming chancer?

My next move, to marry Sheila, would place me right at the heart of the deserving victors over the German criminals. In a sense, I was taking the place of a British man killed in the war.

During these last four years, since July 1944, my only contact with my German past had been through letters. This family correspondence had been a real lifeline through various phases of military confinement. Now I was not really returning home anymore for good. I was returning home as a visitor.

My problem was how to align my English dream with my family in Felsberg in the American zone of occupation in this summer of

1948: all POWs were to be released by the end of May. The release routine was much more formalized now. The only surprise was that our release transport was the first to be paid out in the new German D-Mark, which had just taken the place of the old Reichsmark at 1 to 10. My 666 D-Mark turned out to be far more valuable than the 6,660 Reichsmark I would have received the day before. We were off to Germany with as much luggage as we could carry.

Our new commanding major said to me, 'Schweitzer, you too can stay on as a civilian worker but definitely not as camp leader.' He had always suspected me of being personally behind all the underhand fiddles and transgressions which were practiced with passion. It had become a kind of sport among ourselves to brag about what we had got away with. It was definitely time to be going.

I was home in Felsberg with all my luggage in time for Father's 54th birthday on June 30, 1948.

PART 8

POST-WAR

GERMAN AUSTRIAN ENGLISH

Old Home – New Home

STEPPING OFF THE train at the familiar Gensungen-Felsberg station, I caught my breath. The last time I had been around was the July weekend of 1944, just after the bomb attack on Hitler when I had been called up to Riga. Everything was still much the same as I remembered it, except for a certain worn-down aspect all around. Nobody who knew me was around to notice my unpredicted arrival. Twenty minutes later, I had dragged my luggage to the front door of the doctor's house and knocked.

In no time I was with Dad, Mutti, Tilla, and my siblings, welcomed by all. It was as if the war and POW years were gone, but we were actually older, and we children had grown up. Rosi and Irmi were not even at home anymore. From all the letters between us, except during the lost year 1945, I knew a lot, but now reality hit home.

As the American forces had approached Felsberg in 1945, there had been panic in the town. Mutti had calmly hung out a white sheet as a flag from the town pharmacy's first-floor window when she heard tanks approaching in the morning. Nobody shot at her. The rest of the town followed her example. There was no trouble when American tanks came into the town.

In the following months and years, the problem for survival was food. The farming villages around Felsberg had been denuded of their labour. If the men were alive, they were locked up in camps. The old people and children left behind could only do so much. By working at village farms and using all our garden space to grow vegetables and keep a few hens or rabbits, the family got through. Mutti also kept beehives. Dad and Mutti's brother, Doctor Heinz Roepke, had been early returners from their respective prisoner-of-war camps.

Now I had to join the lines at different offices in the district town of Melsungen to register in order to get my ration and identity cards, to get political clearance, and to apply for an exit visa for my return to England. Father had a casual job at the sugar plant in Wabern, processing sugar beets from farms in the area. When around, I would go with him and earn myself some D-Marks.

As an Austrian citizen wishing to get back to England from the US zone of Germany to study at the LSE and marry Sheila, I was at odds everywhere. The US military government offices in Wiesbaden sat on my application forever. Much needed help came from Ulla Mutti's charming sister-in-law, Aunt Putti, widow of Dr. Juergen Roepke, who had died before his only son Claus was born. A beautiful socialite, she now had a position with the Red Cross in Wiesbaden. She took up my case and got my exit visa to England for January 1949.

Meanwhile I had to face the possibility of not getting back to England. However, my affiliation with the Moral Rearmament movement enabled me to meet Dr. Stein, the Minister of Education of Hessen, who revalidated my 1944 university entrance certificate, thereby enabling my admission in September 1948 in the meantime as a student at the University of Mainz. I had to thank the Allied occupying powers for my preferred treatment as a foreigner, compared with the guilty-nation locals. The occupying powers of Germany made a distinction between 'war-guilty' Germans and 'innocent' foreigners. I had slipped through the net as an Austrian.

For a few months at Mainz, I was thus introduced to the typical German economics of production organization. It was all classroom learning and test papers. Even at the year-end break, I was not sure whether this was my future instead of a new start in London.

The year 1948 became the first Christmas since 1939 celebrated by the whole family together. From 56-year-old Tilla to 10-year-old Heidi, we were all there to usher in the New Year of 1949.

My English Wedding

AS THE CROSS-CHANNEL express drew into Victoria Station, I saw Sheila there waiting on the platform, looking out for me. A minute later, we were in each other's arms. Mother Maggie had a roast beef dinner ready. We then made our provisional home/bedroom in their downstairs front room.

Our wedding was scheduled for the next Saturday, January 29, 1949, at the Fulham Baptist chapel. Sheila went to work at the hospital in the morning, and I made my first trip to the London School of Economics.

I was expected and overwhelmed with papers and programs. I would miss the new-year opening week because Maggie had booked us a week's honeymoon. The whole Moral Armament group came to the wedding. It soon became apparent that we would have to find our own place to live, and I would have to contribute financially to make this viable.

LSE Studies

THE LSE WAS in the process of gaining a worldwide reputation. There was an exhilarating atmosphere around. Being taught scientific knowledge by Austrians Karl Popper and political science by Harold Laski made me think and read widely. Besides the prescribed lecture courses, there were all the other courses and access to eminent visitors' presentations, such as Stigler, Samuelson, and Euken. I had to appear before the Head of Economics, Professor Robbins, and told him my dilemma about full-time study for the degree. He said they were just starting a group of evening students experimentally, who would have to spread their course over an extra year to sit for the final examinations. Would I be prepared to do this? That was all I needed. Now I was off to find a day job, nothing too pretentious to keep my mind clear for evenings at the LSE.

Now John Lewis on Oxford Street gave me a foot in the door, from being a furniture porter to a 'graduate' trainee in the chief accountant's department, with a standard managerial black business suit and pinstriped trousers before I had even graduated. Standardized systems were needed for trading, mechanization, and computers. I had to organize them and regulate the practical performance under Pat Parsons, the often-acting chief accountant.

Through the Fulham Rearmament Association and their secretary, my mother-in-law Maggie Dobinson, I became an adherent of Frank Buchman and his quest for true, peaceful, and patient change.

He embodied what he taught. He did not demand but simply set an example.

We were conventional local Church of England people in Cookham, living among executives at the John Lewis Partnership. Apart from qualifying as a certified accountant, I controversially tried to improve the personal partner relationships at John Lewis in the direction of Frank Buchman's philosophy.

In the summer of 1950, we had our first holiday with the German family in Felsberg. All liked Sheila but regretted that she would make no attempt to get to know German and speak with them. Tilla's fluent English established a warm friendship with her.

Sheila and I gradually grew apart, and during our fairly peaceful divorce, official in 1962, we had an open house, friends, and help from all sides. After this time, Regan and Pete, our two older children, now in their teens, lived with me, and little Catherine, our youngest, was with us most weekends and holidays.

PART 9

FAST FORWARD

My Partnership Career

AT JOHN LEWIS, I incidentally learned that I was a partner, not just an employee, and that the whole organisation was called 'The John Lewis Partnership'. John Spedan Lewis, the founder and current chairman, had just published a book setting out his manifesto. Might I not do better with a job relevant to my studies? Would I not as a partner have a chance to do better? I drafted a letter to the director of personnel, whose offices were provisionally in a nearby backyard, and found a departmental typewriter to borrow for typing it out.

Acting Chief Accountant Mrs. Parsons complimented me on my letter and told me she needed someone to document all the accumulated and often diverging organizational procedures into an up-to-date comprehensive system as a loose-leaf manual of instructions accessible to all partners.

Could I do this? I said: I would love to try. With that, I became a 'graduate' trainee in the chief accountant's department, located across the passage of the personnel department. I would have to wear the standard black business suit with pinstriped trousers, and I would be earning £1,000 per annum, £83 paid monthly. No more cycling to work from Brixton!

The Electronic Age

BY THE EARLY 1960s, IBM electronic computers were tested at John Lewis, and electronics also widened social contacts. Regan and Pete helped me complete questions on the computer dating site about my own personality and other details, and also the qualities I hoped for from the other person. I received three 'eligible' phone numbers. Starting from the top, I met the number-one person in town after work. She was a strong person but had recently slipped off a starting bus, hurting her face. We parted after a polite dinner together. Regan and Pete dared me to try again.

Now I had to meet the young lady in the purple coat at the exit of the Goodge Street tube station. We met and had dinner together in a hotel across the road, chatting cheerfully. It became the true stormy love of our lives. We were so different. Our new life of our joint efforts together grew beyond anything we had ever dared to dream and fear about.

Pam, born in central London, just when German bombers were trying to destroy it, as the only child of her working-class parents, soon became divorced. After school life in a home and a hard short marriage, she was again together with her beloved mother working in a clothing factory when we first met. She was then in good contact with each of her divorced parents, helping them to manage their separate lives. Dad had adopted his grandson, Pam's son, Stephen.

Even while we were courting, Pam raised herself to the top saleslady at a Regent Street fashion store and made herself a house owner in the East End to match this merely home-renting financial manager at the Peter Jones department store in Sloan Square.

Courting Weeks

THERE WERE MANY phone calls and evenings after work get-to-gethers in the following weeks over meals. We also went to the opera and theatre performances at John Lewis-subsidised prices. Then the news: Pam had bought a house in Leytonstone with tenants on the ground floor. She and Mum were busy redecorating the hall and staircase. Soon I got my invitation to stay the night on the upper floor.

The missing links were closed lovingly at Pam's next stay at my rented Mill House in Cookham, Berks. It turned right away into our main joint project: when and how to marry? Sure enough, in Cookham, with the reception at the Odney Country Club on a Saturday. Our 'joint project' was the beginning of many more as life partners in all our full life of ventures.

Our wedding was finally settled for Saturday, August 19, 1967, to take full advantage of the children's school holidays. After the blessing at the Cookham Church, the reception for 60 guests at the Odney Club Boat Room was Pam's triumph as a hostess. Odney Club manager, Brigadier Charlton, welcomed us cheerfully, and then the party continued until late, also including young Stephen, Pam's son.

My car was ready packed for our two-week honeymoon trip across Europe to visit my early life stations, family, and friends. Sunday night we stayed at an Ostend beach hotel. By Tuesday, we arrived in Sterbfritz at the edge of the Roehn Mountains to a great family welcome. Dad's well- remembered English was a great help for Pam. Family and friends came from all over the place.

Back at work, Pam was soon the quality controller of a Regent Street fashion house, and I was the general manager of the novel IBM-computer-animated John Lewis model distribution centre in Stevenage, north of London. We bought our own house there.

Here We Come Germany

OUR FIRST CHILD, our daughter Gretta, was born at the Hitchin Hospital in England in 1971. With our new baby, Pam and I now came to Germany American style, as part of ITT-New York. My first assignment was in Frankfurt, where sister Gittli and her husband Juergen ran their general medical practice in the suburbs. There was an apartment to rent near them, and we spent a pleasant summer there. My parents in Sterbfritz were only a one-hour drive away.

ITT arranged for our family to settle in the Stuttgart area in the American zone of Germany. Sister Gittli was horrified: 'Those Schwabians are so clannish and insular. You will be very much on your own down there.' We found a new house to rent on the fringe of the medieval town of Markgroeningen. Now our German family home in Sterbfritz was two car hours away on the Autobahn.

Pam had been so happy with the doctors and nurses when little Gretta was born at the Hitchin Hospital in England (before we had left for our new job in Germany) that she insisted that our boy should be born there as well a year later. This meant she had to regularly commute back to Britain for check-ups.

Pam's rhesus-negative blood group implication always necessitated an induced birth. As Pam and I were at the Hitchin Hospital birth station on the evening of April 18, 1972, baby Karl was duly born with the help of nurse Mary. Little Karl's christening by our British vicar was celebrated in style in the Markgroeningen Gothic Catholic Church (almost a cathedral). We had a reception in nearby Ludwigsburg, including most members of our wider German family and local friends. Mary then joined us in Markgroeningen as an *au-pair* for the next two years. Pam befriended the British vice-consul and worked as an assistant in the British consulate.

Our furniture from England arrived stuffed full, with ends of dress materials that Pam had cleared out before leaving. On market days, Pam would have a stand selling them in the market calling out '*Eine mark ein meter*'.

Our Clairvoyant

IN 1972 IN Markgroeningen, we held a séance with our young *au pair*, Mary, who was a clairvoyant. Was the real purpose for Mary's 1972 prophecy to hear mother Gritta's message? Were we being forewarned about our Orthodox Jewish conversion in the future? We were gathered around the table with a glass upside down in the middle and the alphabet and numbers in a ring, all placing a finger very lightly on the glass as we started asking questions. The glass moved to spell out the answers. It appeared that Gritta-Mutti was present to communicate with us. Helmut asked about her deathbed and many other things. The voice from the past told us we were going to Afrika, spelt in the German style. Gradually the glass started moving faster and faster, and we all got scared and stopped.

A year later found us ready to move to Johannesburg to work for ITT, an unexpected job transfer.

The Big Move

THE SOUTH AFRICAN government had welcomed our immigration and paid for our journey. The Stuttgart British Consulate gave a leaving party for Pam and a departing staffer. The consul took me aside, saying, 'Don't get me wrong. You have made your decision. I just want to tell you what our official view is about the South African situation. We reckon it will be all over for outsiders there within the next five years.' What could I say, apart from thanking him for telling us? Most people were shaking their heads when they heard of our plans.

Johannesburg was nobody's hometown or tourist target. It was a restless violent centre of influence over wider regions. Its Jan Smuts Airport was the central gate to and from Southern Africa, apart from the distant freight and tourist seaports of Cape Town and Durban.

Johannesburg was still the world leader of gold mining and growing into much wider reaches of business and technical development covering Southern Africa and worldwide connections. Surrounded by Soweto and other black townships, it was however politically constrained by the apartheid Republic of South Africa ruled from Pretoria, Bloemfontein and Cape Town. It would take another 20 years for a peaceful handover to Nelson Mandela's first Black government in 1995. We would be able to play our part in this remarkable transition.

New Year 1975 found us in Johannesburg looking for a suitable home. We would be taken around by estate agents and earmark what we liked. Ron Spies from Spies Real Estate would check it out.

The one-acre property of 51, Knox Street in Waverley, seemed well placed. It was neglected but had potential and a swimming pool. The lady owner, Mrs. Rayner, was desperate to get out, too scared to stay there as a newly single woman on her own. Ron helped us buy the property to move in by May. As a growing family, including Nelly, Pam's mother, and son Stephen, we made this our home for the next 20 years.

Architect Ron Spies and I had continued talking. He offered me a partnership in his expanding business of shopping centres and self-financing hotels around the subcontinent. We accepted his offer. ITT was already on the way down on the New York Stock Exchange.

Settling In

AT THE END of April 1975, Pam, Gretta, and Karl were on their way on the Pendenning Castle, a traditional British passenger boat, to our new South African home. I joined them from its first stop at Cape Town Harbour, where we settled down in a family suite on the boat. It took a pleasant week, calling at Port Elisabeth and East London, to get disembarked at Durban Harbour.

We drove with our car to our Knox Street Johannesburg property with just our suitcases. It was a huge place in comparison to anything we had before. Our freight load of belongings was still on the way to be delivered. Everybody had their own room, but we had to sleep and sit on the floor on blow-up lilos. The bench seats in the breakfast nook left by the previous owner were a blessing.

We were approaching winter at the end of May. In Joburg, more than 1,000 meters above sea level, this meant clear skies, sunny days, and frosty nights. This was not the time to sort out garden areas but to keep warm indoors. In any case, I was tied up working at the struggling Spies Real Estate. I had no idea that in the spring I would be unemployed, job hunting, worrying about losing all we had gained so far, with much time to attend to the outdoor part of our property.

Young Gertrude introduced herself. She had been Mrs. Rayner, the previous owner's maid. She could speak English because she was from Zimbabwe, where English was taught at school. We needed her services. Gretta was not yet 5 years old, and Karl was under 4. Gertrude was familiar with the premises and their upkeep.

Pam checked downtown with a job agency. In no time, she found herself hired as a quality control manager with Phil Arbeter Fashions at his downtown factory.

Security? — What about child-friendly guard dogs? — There must be a pair of them, insisted Pam, just as she had insisted when we had discussed having children six years before. In no time, we owned a pair of boxer puppies, growing up to be powerful, friendly guard dogs as part of the family. They were with us at Knox Street for their whole lives.

Growing Roots at Knox Street

TALKING TO HAROLD Mendelssohn, our northern neighbour across the fence, I learned that both Harold and his wife Pinky were keen tennis players and hosted a men's doubles round of friends every Sunday morning on their court. What a chance to play tennis again!

Up to 1971 in England, I had been the honorary chairman of the London Business Houses Tennis league, playing summer and winter tournaments, and also chairman of the Odney Tennis Club in the Berkshire league. For the last five years, we had been all over the place with little chance for regular tennis.

This was social tennis: two doubles sets before tea and one or two more sets afterwards, depending on the conversation. Harold was the most senior of us. He had served as a private in the South African division of the British army for the whole war on the North African front under Montgomery's command. Half a century ago, we would have been on opposite sides during a terrible war. All the rest of us men were graduate professionals. Was he the only one who had done war service? I was the odd non-Jew, but otherwise fitted in. All of us were insured by Liberty Life through Harold.

As a family, we started road running with a group of volunteers. It had become a new fashionable exercise. I was the only one who persevered because I was determined to run a marathon of 41.5 km. I was training then on Saturdays with the Jewish Happy Road

Runners group until we were beginning our future Orthodox conversion. Eventually I ran my only marathon in a race around the East Rand mining areas two years later in 3 hours 59 minutes. On the run, I persisted only in the certainty that Pam was expecting me at the next checkpoint. I collapsed at the end. That was the end of my long-distance running.

Meanwhile Gretta persevered with her ballet training and took up ice skating. Both she and Karl were perfecting their swimming. I found our pool too short for proper swimming, but we all took to swimming in the Warmbaths' hot spring waters a couple of hours' drive away.

Within a year, the worldwide economic crisis had also ended Spies Real Estate. I joined the stock-exchange-listed PG-Glass Group for the rest of my executive life until age 65. By that time, this Jewish family concern had expanded to become Glass South-Africa with worldwide subsidiaries. Pam had thrived in the local fashion industry, which was then being decimated by cheap Asian imports.

At school, our children were regular winners at the swimming galas. The key to their accomplishment was really that they had been taught to swim well earlier in their lives than the others. In their case, it had been a much bigger part of growing as a person than just practicing a new skill.

On our first year-end camp with the caravan club, we camped near a small lake in the Drakensberg Mountains. A swimming race was announced for all school kids right across the lake, a 60-meter distance. The parents watching got quite alarmed when they saw little Gretta and Karl taking the lead swimming more under the water than on top. Were they drowning, trying to survive? No, they were just swimming their best way in order to win.

Clear as Glass

CHANGING JOBS AT age 50 has implications of final choice and chance. PG-Glass was listed on the Johannesburg Stock Exchange, but Express Glass halfway down Main Street looked more like a trading outlet than a head office. It was, in fact, a trading branch on the ground floor. The head office was crammed onto the first floor of the front building. John, the personnel manager, had his own cubicle.

He explained that the group had been expanding all over Southern Africa, with branches everywhere from Cape Town to Zambia and from Namibia to Malawi and Mozambique, dealing and installing building and motor glass. The main glass supplier was the Pilkington Float Glass plant on the East Rand. It would be the organisation and method manager's task to get it all efficiently running and coordinated.

John had no doubt about my qualifications. The final word would, however, be with Ronnie Lubner, the CEO, who was out of town. When I was called in to see Ronnie three weeks later, I was confirmed, which did not mean I had an office, but I got a car to get around and desk space where I could find one. Whenever Ronnie did branch visits, I was part of the party. Otherwise, I made my own way and arrangements.

In this fluid expansive environment, driven by the takeover master, Ronnie Lubner, there was a great need for organization and methods for a combined advantage. Ronnie asked me to meet him in Los

Angeles, USA, for the takeover of the West Coast Glass Group in order to resume talks after an aborted attempt many years earlier.

In due course, the takeover deal went through, financed in the USA. It paved the way for future PG takeover expansions under Ronnie's initiatives.

While on a trip to Denver, Colorado, Ronnie called me from LA, telling me that I should rush to take a plane back home. Pam was in hospital after a back operation. She had not forewarned me in case it might spoil my job prospects.

Two days later, I got back to Joburg via Reykjavik and London to Pam's hospital bedside. Now it was my turn to marvel at Pam's amazing recovery capability, which also delighted the hospital team. Pam, in turn, was amazed that her factory boss, Phil Arbiter, personally visited her in hospital. Meeting him there at the evening visiting times, we became enduring family friends.

All the while Gertrude had calmly looked after little Gretta and Karl at our spacious, half-empty Waverly home.

Figure 27 - Family Picture, Johannesburg (Left to Right: Gretta, Pam, Helmut, Karl)

Waverly Shul

IN ALL THE six years we had been living on Knox Street, Waverley in Johannesburg, we had hardly taken note of the big Orthodox synagogue complex around the bottom end of the street. It must be a very exclusive society, we thought.

We were both frantically busy professionally. Pam was a factory manager for one of the large Jewish fashion houses. I, as organisation and method manager of the Plate Glass Group, had just registered for the 1981-1984 part-time MBA course in the WITS-Business School.

Figure 28 - MBA Graduation at Wits Business School, Johannesburg

Gretta, aged 10, and Karl, aged 9, were getting to the end of their local primary school. Each also had their own newspaper delivery round. Stephen at 18 was facing his matric finals at the local state high school.

We had come to South Africa in 1975 under the control of the ruling hard-line right-wing conservative apartheid government, which was resisting the inevitable handover of power to the Black majority with brute force. We felt like the pragmatic Jewish businesspeople with whom we were now working. We were with them in their practical, positive approach to the inevitable future.

In the hard times of Pam's youth in the East End of London, Jews had helped her when she was in need. Now Orthodox Waverley Shul had psychologists voluntarily on call to help needy souls, irrespective of their origins and beliefs. Pam was amazed and phoned the organizers to wish them well. She had a talk with Angela Marcus, the Rebbetzin (Rabbi's wife), who then organized a meeting for us with her husband, Rabbi Barry Marcus, about the possibility of our converting to Judaism.

Rabbi Marcus took us seriously and set out an immediate approach: take it or leave it. He gave us a good idea of what it meant to become an Orthodox Jew. We would have to prove our eligibility by conduct and learning.

Rabbi Marcus was not much concerned about my German past. He accepted us as a family.

It was up to us to fit in. There were a lot of conditions for us, most of which would be life changing. The children would have to switch over to Yeshiva College, the private Jewish high school in Glenhazel a couple miles away. He would arrange their admission. We, the whole family, were expected to honour Shabbat from now on and attend the shul services as from the coming Friday evening. No driving, no technology, no telephone, no activating electricity, and no cooking on the holy Shabbat.

We sat down with the children to discuss the implications of this. Stephen had reservations about joining. He was busy preparing for his final high school matriculation and did not want to become 'part of the kids'. Gretta (10) and Karl (9) felt ready to do better.

Dusk the following Friday evening found us four in our best outfits walking down to our first Shabbat evening service. How would this great Jewish congregation feel about this past German interloper? How could I (with my past) dare to face them?

Suddenly I was shaken by an amazing exaltation, a burst of gratitude and happiness like the one that had gripped me the first time I stepped on English soil. We had been invited in, given a chance to prove ourselves. We had to do our best to deserve it. We had to take our chance with open arms. So, we did. We were welcome. Karl was charging around with the boys. Gretta made friends and babysat for the Marcus family. Pam joined the ladies' guild, and I joined the volunteer security guards, and later, the Shul Committee. All of us had to learn service observance and Hebrew. For Gretta and Karl, this was part of their schooling. We 'oldies' had to be on our toes to keep up with them, making sense of it as we went along, backing it up with self-study.

We were in good company. Many of our fellow congregants were new to the faith and were new to observant practice as we were. We became part of a wider Jewish religious revival. Shabbat as a definite day of rest, peace, and hospitality came to us as a revelation. We became a family together with friends. It truly became 'our re-creation'.

The Jewish Revival

WE WERE IN the company of second- and third-generation immigrant Jewish families from Tsarist Russia and the rest of the pogrom-filled life in Eastern Europe, mostly Lithuanian. On arrival, they had much in common with the Bible-traditional Afrikaner settlers but also with the British mining and colonizing innovators, not to speak of the Marxists and idealists working with the African revolutionaries. Good - the Jews were still subject to antisemitism from both British and Afrikaners but were positioned between all of these ideologies and had no direct clashes with either. All around, Jews were now a steadying influence against outbursts of blind and criminal violence. Jews predominated in the growing legal and medical professions and contributed to the economy in business and in welfare movements, donating to charities, academic professions, and universities. Much of big business was free from the actual governing civil infrastructure.

This Jewish revival was animated after the war by the foundation of Jewish elite schools linked with Orthodox synagogues. Their graduates were now enlivening shul observance. State schools were increasingly filling with black and coloured pupils. Private Jewish high schools were becoming a refuge for children, even from conventional Jewish families.

All these changes were augmented by the growing big city attractions. The post-war Jewish generations moved up from the provinces, particularly to Johannesburg and Pretoria. Jewish communities up-country faded. Only in coastal Cape Town, Durban Port Elizabeth could Jewish communities manage to hold their own.

There were also overseas dynamics. Israel was gathering in returners but also contributing ex-patriates. Commonwealth countries such as Australia, Britain, and Canada became South Africans' exodus destinations but also sources of active arrivals. The United States was always a special connection. This was not just one-way escape-route traffic. Enterprising Israelis, Britons, and Americans were also on the move in and around.

Part of this turnaround was started by the ebullient American Rabbi Avraham Tanzer and his family. Glenhazel grew into something like a spiritual home of the new-generation Jews, challenging the traditional chief rabbis and institutions edging north to Sandton, west of Louis Botha Avenue.

Central Johannesburg was gradually turning into more of a no-go area for white people. The city shuls and hallmarks were gradually abandoned and replaced by new sites.

Our Orthodox Learning Curve

AT THE SHUL, you could always pick up a prayer book (1,200-page volumes) and a Chumash (the 1,300-page Bible), with Hebrew text and an English translation on the facing pages, and with helpful notes all along. These books stayed at the shul. We learners certainly needed to have our own copies at home to study. Pam and I had rabbinic supervisors give us tasks to read and absorb to acquire and test our general knowledge for getting *magied* (converted) and elected as Jews to be members of our congregation in Waverly. This process was coordinated and led by the Johannesburg *Beth Din*, the Jewish legal court composed of three senior rabbis.

For young Gretta and Karl, all this was also part of their daily schooling. Soon they were telling us parents what the rules were. Occasionally, the *Beth Din* wanted to meet and question the whole family together. Towards the end of our third year, all four of us were standing once more in the forecourt of the *Beth Din* building in downtown Johannesburg, waiting for our turn. Chief Rabbi Casper walked out of his adjoining office on his way home for the day and noticed us standing there. What were we waiting for? Before I could open my mouth, Karl faced him saying that every time we had been to meet the *Beth Din*, we had been told to come back again next time. He was now getting due for his *bar mitzvah*. We were quaking in our shoes. The chief rabbi was an imposing person, and we would never have dared to speak to him so directly. He did not seem to be bothered.

Chief Rabbi Casper asked for our notice paper and told us to wait. He came back a little while later, telling Karl and us that we would now be confirmed with our Jewish names. This was the official event for all of us. This meant my induction at the shul, wearing for the first time a tallis, the white mantle of male membership worn around the shoulders, and getting called up to the Hebrew Torah reading from the holy scrolls.

Now as regulars of Waverly Shul, we were soon part of the community. Rabbi Marcus invited us to dinner at his home next to the shul. Gretta had fun playing with their young children. She soon became their child minder when the rabbi and Angela wanted to go out to functions.

I invited the rabbi to a game of tennis on our scarcely used new court. He chased me around the court with his powerful game. So much for the ex-chairman of the London Business Houses Tennis league. My tennis was, however, a fit for the Sunday morning doubles sessions next door in Harold Mendelsohn's court with a lively group of his business friends. They were not Waverly Orthodox.

Pam played her part in the shul's ladies' guild, renowned for their exceptional catering services. I was soon part of the volunteer guards safeguarding the premises from intruders during services.

Now on to the next step: getting married! The law required us to get married in conformity with Jewish law this time. For us, who had been married 15 years with six children, this was a really special experience.

Our Jewish wedding was arranged by Waverley Shul on the shul forecourt on the 15th of Kislev 5745, Sunday December 9, 1984, under the mid-summer sun. Later, we would become known by our Jewish names, Yitzchak and Rivka, the devoted Biblical married couple that were the offspring of founding father Abraham.

Figure 29 - Our Jewish Marriage Certificate (Ketubah)

Figure 30 - Now Yitzchak and Rivka: Our Jewish Wedding with Rabbi
Marcus

Karl was one of the pole holders of the *chupa* (wedding canopy).
His *bar mitzvah* and Jewish adult status had to wait until a free mid-
June Sabbath in 1985, well after his actual 13th birthday in mid-April
because all the available dates had been booked up well in advance.
Gretta had missed her chance of a *bat mitzvah* a year earlier. She was
now our most integrated Jewish family member, with great friendships
and the star pupil of Natali's ballet dancing class across the way. Natali
was Naty Aremband's daughter, the shul's maintenance manager,
with whom I sat in the shul behind the *bima*, the main podium. Naty
was my constant and sure guide through the intricacies of devotional
services with his telling sign language.

Gretta also made her mark at the Yeshiva College girls' college by
promoting game activities. We became sponsors of the Net Ball cup
(women's basketball). As head girl of the school in her final year there,

Gretta worked with the head boy, Doron Perez. Pam, as a member of the ladies' guild, worked best with his mother, Gail, providing all meals and refreshments. I, as a keen attendant of management conferences and courses, kept getting together with Gil, his father, who was also with Waverly Shul. Once the penny dropped that we were all the same families, we became great family friends.

Gil and Gail's three sons and a daughter were all set on settling in Israel.

By 2016, we ourselves had moved to London to be with our daughter Gretta and her family.

PART 10

LATE LIFE PERSPECTIVES

Family Reunion in Gneixendorf

IT WAS WEDNESDAY, August 30, 2017. Rivka and I were standing in the dark before the Colping residential house of Krems University at 1am, figuring out how to get in. Earlier in the evening, we had flown from London to the Vienna Airport and then set out in a red Skoda car towards Krems, finding our way in the night through Vienna along the Donau Kanal, and then through all the south-of-the-river places in a westerly direction. What took us less than two hours, had taken Ludwig van Beethoven and his nephew Karl two wintry days when they returned via this route to Vienna from Gneixendorf on Saturday, December 2, 1826. Their impetuous journey, with Ludwig in a towering rage after a serious disagreement with his brother, Johann, had taken place in an open milk cart; this became the great composer's death warrant on March 26, 1827.

Colping House had been booked for our 2017 German family reunion over the coming weekend, partly because Schloss Gneixendorf or the *Wasserhof* had been the home of the Kleyle/Schweitzers for 88 years and three generations from 1847 to 1935. Johann van Beethoven, the composer's younger brother, had owned the estate earlier from 1819 to 1836.

Gneixendorf has since become the northern end of the city of Krems. Krems and the Wachau area of the Danube River are now a United Nations World Heritage site.

Chronik der Familie von Schweitzer

1847-1945

Gneixendorf

Postkarte vom Schloss Gneixendorf, ehemals der Wasserhof erbaut 1200, 2007 ein Sanierungsobjekt

Familientreffen am 12. 10. 2007 in Landal Coldenhof Holland

Figure 31 - Schloss Gneixendorf (2007)

In June 2008, I had been with sister Rosemarie to Gneixendorf as guests of honour for the celebration of the 100-year anniversary of the village church and the 40-year anniversary of the final integration of Gneixendorf with the city of Krems. Our family had been always at home in the village, and we had kept coming back to visit and see the graves over the years. The Schweitzers had donated the land to the church. Dad, as mayor and the largest employer, had been the respected 'Herr Baron' after World War I. Otherwise, university professor Rosemarie from Germany, and I, Helmut from Johannesburg, would not have been invited for the occasion. The mayoress of Krems, the vicar, and I had to speak to the crowd. I told them my own Beethoven story.

Gneixendorf Restored

LATER WEDNESDAY MORNING, we drove up to Gneixendorf. Mother's grave in the little graveyard across from the Beethoven memorial looked well cared for. Eighty-two-year-old Frau Messner came over to talk to us. We had not met before. She promised to water our grave whenever she was watering the Messner graves.

We drove across to the Schloss with its big square clock tower. In 2008, it had become derelict, uninhabitable. Now, in 2017, it looked splendid behind a new white outer wall with a big Beethoven plate glass memorial on view. This was the work of Viennese architect Ernst Linsberger, who had bought the ruined buildings for his foundation.

Our father, Otto, had sold the estate in 1935, when the farm could not sustain the family any more following the financial world crisis. Three years later after Austria had become the German *Ostmark*, the German Wehrmacht had taken over the estate as a military base, which during the war was extended to become the largest prisoner-of-war camp for some 66,000 POWS, most of whom were posted out to labour around the country. The fairly flat highland also lent itself to building an airdrome, progressively reducing the area left for farming.

From 1945 to 1955, the Soviet Russian occupying forces had taken over. Eventually what was left was returned to survivors of the Feichtinger family, who had lost everything during the war. Unable to restore the premises, they had no choice but to occupy them as long as they would not collapse.

For the villagers, all of this had been the most bewildering experiences of their lives. What was left of the farming land was grabbed by the village farming families after the war. For a time, the unemployed could earn money digging up the bodies of dead POWs for transfer to their home countries or mass graves in Krems.

We rang the new gate bell of what had now become 'Schloss Wasserhof'. After giving our names to a questioning voice, the side gate was opened to us. We crossed the courtyard to the tower entrance and into the pillared ground floor hall with a new glass-fronted office on the side. There we met the tall, distinguished, whitehaired master architect, Ernst Linsberger. He proudly showed us what had already been done and outlined to us what was yet to come to make the whole built up area into a creative artists' centre, funded by a range of formidable international foundations.

Figure 32 - Restored Schloss (2017)

Linsberger's reconstruction had homed in on the interior and exterior of the original building from around 1550. This had been overlaid by a revamp following the dissolution of the Catholic abbeys during Napoleon's reign up to 1813. This overlaid image was what we remembered from our childhood, and painters and photographers had recorded them. This restored mansion appeared familiar, and yet, strangely more ancient. The clock of the tower was gone, but the sun- dial of the south face stood out again.

All the outbuildings were still grey silhouettes, including the giant, ancient *schuettkasten* (storage court) where in the pre-Napoleonic centuries the villagers had to deliver their tenths of produce to the land-owning monasteries. Reluctantly, Linsberger led us into this massive structure. During the Russian occupation, a group of East German artists had occupied it and painted the first pillared hall walls, floor, and ceiling in most diverting, semi-abstract themes. Much of it had already faded over the years.

Linsberger gave us a hard look. 'You must realise, these historic buildings had not been maintained for generations'. I thought to myself that Dad at least added a lightning conductor on the shingle roof. Linsberger assured us that all buildings would be restored according to his plan, mostly as artists' studios.

Modern standard living quarters were already well-advanced opposite to the south side of the Schloss-Strasse. Jokingly, he added, in the future he might have the capacity to host our complete family reunion crowd. In parting, he added that he might act as our guide when we were due to come as a family group at 10 am over the weekend.

Pam and I left the image of Linsberger's enthusiasm to look at the competing Beethoven house across the way. Despite its past

strident presence on the internet, we found it closed up, dilapi-
dated, and abandoned as far as one could see through the breaks
in the wall.

Lengenfeld Revisited

WE NOW JOURNEYED along our intended weekend route past the wilderness left of the POW camp on to Lengenfeld via Stratzing village. Here the graveyard is way outside the village with the Schweitzer mausoleum in the middle. It would be the site of remembrance led by our family priest, Claus-Juergen. It seemed to be waiting for us. Buried here are our Schweitzer great-grand- parents and Aunt Emmy. The idea was to remember all who could not be with us this time here.

Down in the village at the crossroads, we found the Schloss with its four-corner crumbling turrets complete but abandoned. We walked around the locked premises. The grounds were tidy. Not a soul around. On the locked front entrance was an old notice from 2013 of an invitation to the owner's funeral service at the graveyard chapel. Time seemed to have stood still here.

We also checked the way to Dross village, where our organisers, Claus-Juergen and son Markus Roepke, had booked a late meal and wine tasting. This locale was closed, with the owners still on leave. So were the homes of personal friends in Gneixendorf. It was astonishing how everywhere vineyards had taken the place of traditional fields. It reminded me of the rather amusing story of my own vineyard.

According to the Schweitzer tradition, it would have been my turn to become a Doctor of Law. In 1931, a surprised aunt Tilla wrote in her diary: 'Young Helmut tells me he is not going to be a medical doctor and not a Doctor of Law'. As it happened, she was right.

Our Golden Anniversary and
The Family Reunion 2017

BY COINCIDENCE, PAM and I had just celebrated our 50-year golden wedding anniversary in London. We were going to retrace part of our honeymoon of 1967, which had been a round trip from the Thames to the Danube, visiting the sites of my youth. Now, 50 years later, we were back again, waiting for our extended family reunion.

By Wednesday evening, cousin Claus' son, Markus, had arrived from Munich with his linguist daughter and photographer, Magdalena, and his boat-builder son, Quirin, both champions of the media. As usual, Pam had organised special bags for all the adults with useful contents. Thursday was the day of arrival for the rest, totalling just over 50 people ranging over four generations. Claus-Juergen, sister Irmgard, and I were the only ones left of the pre-war generation. Eight of us had already been born post-2000.

The confined public facilities of the Colping house, where we were staying, brought everybody together, helping mutual encounters. However, the really lively spirit of this weekend was surely the sum of everybody's contribution. The English-German language barriers were overcome. It was the heartiest family reunion so far. Ulla Mutti and Rosemarie would have loved it if only they could have been there.

The round trip to the villages, mansions, and graveyards together was achieved in 14 cars. Architect Linsberger welcomed us nicely

Figure 33 - Gneixendorf Family Reunion (2017)

but, facing our restless German-English crowd, withdrew to leave us to our own devices around the buildings. Then we found the rival Beethoven *Trautinger Hof*, which had belonged to the Kneifl family, open, trying to sell apples and nuts. We pushed our way in and were readily admitted to see for ourselves how the site had worked before the present generation had moved out from their unmaintained mansion. Between them, these two opposite properties had taken turns to serve as the Gneixendorf Beethoven site. Now the revived Schloss *Wasserhof* project, with its new Beethoven memorial plate, had become the uncontested site.

The abandoned Schloss Lengenfeld was now successfully broken into by our youngsters and inspected in its bare left-over state. Neither of the two Georgs ever settled there for good. Only the Kleyle/ Schweitzer ancestors and Aunt Emmy had found their undisturbed resting place at the mausoleum in the graveyard outside the village. Aunt Emmy had been the ultimate guardian of the Schloss that had never actually belonged to her husband and had not devolved to me.

PART 11

WHAT NOW?

Family Reunion

THE 2017 FAMILY reunion was conceived and organised by the Roepkes around the last corners of the still-visible family history, which was connected to them only by our beloved Ulla Mutti. We ex-Austrians are immensely grateful to the Roepkes for this. In these times of rampant family mobility, historical sites are becoming a thing of the past. It was the most memorable reunion so far.

Claus-Juergen and I are now left as the last living family-wide representatives with long memories and connections. Now back in London after 42 years in South Africa, I can be in better touch in all directions, English and German, past and present.

Over the last years, I have concentrated on preparing myself for such a task by researching a family-wide biography, how our clan has survived and grown in the 20th century through two World Wars on the losing side for a more hopeful future.

Recent History

OUR ORIGINAL PLANS to live in Israel were put on hold by our children. Since she had been born in England and was the holder of a British passport, Gretta wanted to emigrate to the UK. Husband Mark also had family living in England. They both felt their autistic son, Daniel, would have better opportunities for his special education. Daughter Deanna went to the same Jewish high school. While we were still in South Africa, we established a regular annual visit to our children in London over the Pesach holidays, which enabled us to prepare for our emigration back to England in 2016. Gretta's home is now our trigenerational family residence in Edgeware, London, in which we have our own apartment.

Karl, on the other hand, landed up in Perth, Australia, where he married Dr. Jennii, from a Jewish Australian family with a strong Jewish community affiliation. There they have happily established themselves with their two daughters.

Our Current Jewish
Life in London

ON ARRIVING IN our new location in Edgeware, London after leaving South Africa, our first priority was to establish ourselves within a Jewish community. We joined the big Edgeware Shul, but also found a home from home within smaller communities nearby that had a large ex-South African membership. Rivka immediately established herself in the welfare services and then became a trained *shomer* or food supervisor for the London *Beth Din*, where she works at present. Wherever she goes, she has been appreciated for her competence and helpfulness.

I had a particularly strong connection with Rabbi Lord Jonathan Sacks, the late Chief Rabbi. I had met him in South Africa but did so again in London. I followed his interesting *shiurim* and lectures wherever possible, which were always very enlightening and inspiring, and read many of his extensive writings.

The present Chief Rabbi, Sir Ephraim Mervis, is an ex-South African, and we have met on several occasions, during which we shared our common experiences.

During our time in London, Gretta's two children celebrated their *bar/bat mitzvahs*. We went to Israel to share this happy occasion. It took place in natural surroundings with the ancient archaeology of the land of Israel's surroundings and planted trees at Neot Kedumim.

I recently testified at the United States Holocaust Memorial Museum for six one-hour sessions, which are up on their website of oral testimony. I also had the opportunity to speak a couple of times at Limud. This is a yearly conference that is a Jewish exchange of knowledge by highly respected professionals to the younger generation, a natural intergenerational meeting. As a speaker, I lectured on different subjects, most recently sharing my life story, which the attendees were very interested in. I have also arranged to bequest my personal and family documents, photographs, and artifacts, as well as my German-related books, to the Wiener Library in London.

Figure 34 - Second Barmitzvah in London at Age 96 (2022)

Last year, 2022, our London Jewish life was celebrated in commemorating my 'second *bar mitzvah*' at age 96. My first *bar mitzvah* had taken place in 2009 in South Africa, at 83, in recognition of having become Jewish and counting from the biblical allotment of three score and ten of 70 years old. Rivka created a very special occasion in a friend's garden and put up a marquee. People came from all parts of Edgeware to participate in this momentous occasion. Our morning services took place outside on the terrace to accommodate all our visitors. I was called up to the Torah to read my portion, and I could look back at nearly 40 years of being Jewish, feeling very much like I belonged. It was a really joyful occasion,

Figure 35 - Yitzchak, London, February 2023

with tables decorated with balloons in blue and white as a tribute to the Israeli flag. My real birthday in 1926 in Gneixendorf 96 years earlier had fortuitously presaged my future Jewish identity, as it coincided with the future momentous occasion of the founding of the State of Israel in 1948. Or perhaps it was not a coincidence at all but a sign of things to come.

APPENDICES

IN THEIR OWN WORDS

Serena's Story 2002 to 2023

I ARRIVED IN Los Angeles to join Serena, our close friend from Johannesburg, and her family for her son's *bar mitzvah* and her daughter's wedding, which were taking place on the same long weekend of the New Year at the end of 2002. After our celebratory Friday night dinner with all their guests in the hall of a nearby shul, Serena and I were strolling back together to where we were staying. Serena asked me about my experience of becoming an Orthodox Jew. I started to tell the story of my youth, and Serena's response was so enthusiastic that I began to feel this was worth writing and perhaps publishing. I began writing my story, which I have been doing ever since. Back in London, after 42 years in south Africa, such experiences as to how our clan was formed and grew to face the upheavals of the 20th century through two World Wars lost by Germany, have become the survivor's task to tell: now or never.

Having generated hundreds of pages of short essays, each one focusing on part of the bigger narrative as I began to write more rigorously, I realized that this story was an impossible one — a young soldier and nominal war criminal who had enlisted in the Waffen SS. We had sworn an oath to 'render unconditional obedience to Adolf Hitler, the *Fuhrer* of the German Reich and its people, supreme commander of the armed forces, and will be ready as a brave soldier to risk my life at any time for this oath'. Now I suddenly saw my chance to see the context of my story in a wider framework. Serena thought it was unique. Here we were walking together as Jews talking about my past experiences. Now my reluctance to think about my past life changed. I had to find my own future. Many coincidences have helped me. For example, my English had enabled me to become the go-between after the war in the American and British POW camps. I was accepted as a trusted interpreter.

I realized that there was a more than ordinary connection between our original meeting in Johannesburg as part of the Jewish community and our post-South African life, now as Jewish friends celebrating this family *simcha* in Los Angeles together.

Karl's Story,
in His Own Words

Embracing Change: A Family's
Journey to Judaism

MY CHILDHOOD TOOK an unexpected turn when my parents, then Helmut and Pam, decided to convert to Judaism while we were living in Johannesburg, South Africa. I was around 10 years old, and as most children would, I initially resisted the changes — the new rules, traditions, and even a new school. However, the warm embrace of the Waverly shul and the welcoming community helped me adjust to our new way of life. The long walks on Shabbat soon became cherished family moments.

I found solace in the nurturing environment of my new religious school, and it wasn't long before I simply saw myself as Jewish, never questioning my identity again. While my upbringing was deeply rooted in this faith, my religious commitment has waxed and waned over the years. Despite that, my father's courageous journey and the choices my parents (now Yitzchak and Rivka) made have shaped the person I am today.

Now, as a proud husband and father of two beautiful daughters, I look back on our family's transformation with gratitude. Our journey has brought me to where I am now — a part of a happy Jewish family, bonded by love and a shared history. My father's story is a testament to resilience, growth, and the power of embracing change.

Rivka's Story,
in Her Own Words

GROWING UP IN Old Street, City Road, London, I went to a church
school, St. Lukes, just up the road from where my family lived. Every
Sunday morning, I went to 'The Leyshen Mission' across the road.
I never really felt like I belonged. The feeling of not belonging continued for most of my younger years. I tried the Catholic Church
and the Methodist Church, but none of them felt right. I even went
to see a rabbi on Mile End Road, but was told 'read this, read that'.
Unfortunately, that is not my style; I needed a more practical approach,
as I am a hands-on person.

This is why Rabbi Marcus in Johannesburg was so good for me.
At the *Beth Din*, whatever they told me to do, I did. If my head was
to be covered, I ran to buy a hat. Looking at other women at shul,
I was surprised that even the rabbi's wife had no head covering. Then
I discovered that their hair was in fact a wig. My first time coming
home with one on my head, Mum had a fit: 'Oh no Pam, you have
cut your hair!'

I was proud to be accepted as a Jew, even whilst only converting.
Only recently, through a DNA testing kit I discovered that I am
50% Ashkenazi Jewish. This felt like wow amazing…until I realized
that maybe my dad was not really my dad. Now through my son
and the '23 and Me' DNA test, I have found I have a half-brother

and a half-sister, and my dad was a Cohen. No wonder I struggled as a child!

Our conversion gave us Hebrew names. Changing and using our Hebrew names only happened after I almost died on an operating table. I had said for many years that I would die before I was 64.

I went under anaesthesia saying the *Shema* and woke up thinking I did not say the wayfarer's prayer. Since that time, we have been permanently known by these names, Rivka and Yitzchak.

This, hand in hand with my beloved Yitzchak, has been my journey.

Epilogue

I WANTED TO write this book as a way for future generations to learn from nearly a century of experience. Responding to the unexpected events of my life took me on a different path. I was planning to be an academic, but world events overtook these plans. In retrospect, many potentially miraculous events in my life pointed to Judaism in a consistent pattern redirecting our connections.

Meeting Rivka was the turning point in our Jewish future. Her shared life story and her connection with Judaism from a young age steered our concerns towards this major change. In retrospect, becoming Jewish was the outcome of many different shared experiences. We felt we were being led unconsciously until we were in the full process of immersion in Jewish life. Now we play our part as Jews, finding a good purpose and life with all our Jewish family and friends. Finding so many people that we could surround ourselves with felt natural. We were both in this together as a partnership. I was worried about the practical steps of becoming Jewish. I felt I was a potential suspect to these Jewish friends who politely did not ask searching questions. We were odd intruders in actual fact. But this did not in any way become a serious issue.

The general attitude towards Germans was voiced by Rivka's mum when she was told about our first date. She burst out, 'He fought on the wrong side!' She warmed up to me when we met face to face, and her reservations vanished. She later lived in South Africa with us when we became Jewish. She worked in a Jewish old age home and made friends there; they had to employ two people to replace her.

I was personally worried because we were so much welcomed that I could not quite believe it. This was unusual in my British German family life. My last name was a kind of problem. I was even more concerned about hostility because "German" was obviously a word that meant rejection. I had my Austrian excuse of course, and as soon as people knew it was Austrian and not German, the climate became much warmer. It made a tremendous difference. Personally, I had always had a special relationship with the rabbis wherever we were, including the chief rabbis, as a kind of exception in a sense, a welcome perception. Having made a rather daring attempt to become Jewish, we were respected rather than suspected. Rivka always led the way. Having Jewish children was Rivka's mission.

Walking into shul, the hidden suspect spoiling the picture, I felt regret for being involved with the past. I have stayed Austrian because I was born that way. I had mutual understandings with Austrians that I did not have on the German side. The major exception to this was my German stepmother.

In conclusion, looking back on this memoir, nothing can be more fitting to describe my journey than this phrase written by Lord Rabbi Jonathan Sacks, the late Chief Rabbi of Britain:

"We cannot change the past. But by changing the way we think about the past, we can change the future." [1]

---

1   Covenant and Conversation: Studies in Spirituality Vayigash, Reframing (Rabbi Sack's Covenant and Conversation www.rabbisacks.org/covenant-conversation/vayigash/reframing/

Figure 36 - Manuscript Finished.............. Cheers!

Printed in Great Britain
by Amazon